PRAISE FOR *CLOSE FOR LIFE*
AND JOSH CADILLAC

Josh Cadillac is a whirlwind of inspiration in the real estate industry. He argues that by starting with the appropriate mindset and exhibiting credibility, professionalism, and a deep understanding of your customer's needs, anyone who has the passion and dedication can become successful. Consider this very readable gem your own personal playbook to guide you on your journey.

> —**Dr. Laurence J. Pino, Esq.**, founder and CEO
> of Tuscan Gardens

An indispensable book for any real estate agent (or salesperson, for that matter)! This will now be part of our annual renewal training!

> —**Leigh Brown**, ABR, AHWD, CDPE, CRS, CIPS,
> CLHMS, CyberStar, EcoBroker, ePRO, MilRES,
> SRES, President of NC REALTORS®, and
> board member of the REALTORS® Relief Foundation

Josh Cadillac is among the finest real estate educators anywhere, and in *Close for Life*, he shares his wealth of knowledge with the world. Informative, meaningful, and impactful, this book is the definitive guide for anyone who is serious about a career in real estate.

> —**Richard L. Barbara, Esq.**, counsel at Barreto Group
> and CFO of Coral Gables Title + Escrow, LLC

In *Close for Life*, Josh Cadillac gifts real estate professionals with an invaluable how-to on building a loyal client base for life. A true necessity in today's competive marketplace.

> —**Richard H. Burch**, CRB, CRS, GRI, ePro, TRC,
> AHWD, and founder of Burch & Associates
> International, LLC

I have worked with tens of thousands of agents over the years; yet I have never met anyone who is better trained in the real estate space than Josh Cadillac. Josh has dedicated his life to making real estate agents smarter, and in *Close for Life*, he delivers a master class on how to win big and build a thriving career. This book is chock-full of practical advice to help you be at the top of your game. The stories that Josh weaves throughout are so captivating, it's hard to put the book down! Required reading for all real estate agents.

　　—**Knolly Williams**, The Business Healer, author of *Success*
　　with Listings and *3 Hours a Day*

Close for Life is a must-read for anyone in any business. Josh explains in no-nonsense terms how, in a sea of epidemic unreliability and self-serving greed, you can easily stand head and shoulders above the rest as the trusted authority.

　　—**Jeff Wright**, CEO of Agent Sales Group

In *Close for Life*, Josh equips real estate agents with the insights and tools they need to build a successful, trustworthy, knowledgeable, client-centric business. He provides the building blocks to become an authority in the real estate field and, most importantly, a process to win and retain clients for a lifetime. This book is highly recommended to new and seasoned agents who want to get a full picture of the right way to build a real estate career.

　　—**Eric Anderson** and **Noelle Frieson** of The Center for
　　Real Estate Education

Engaging, entertaining, and informative, *Close for Life* is an excellent book for those who want to improve their business. The practical tips and advice Josh Cadillac offers are easy to understand and implement. One of the book's strengths is that it covers multiple aspects of selling, from mindset to knowledge to tactics. This makes it a comprehensive guide that is suitable for both beginners and experienced salespeople.

　　—**Kunal Seth**, cofounder of The Seth Brothers

CLOSE *for* LIFE

CLOSE *for* LIFE

THE REAL ESTATE AGENT'S GUIDE TO CREATING SATISFIED CUSTOMERS THAT ONLY DO BUSINESS WITH YOU

JOSH CADILLAC

Mc
Graw
Hill

NEW YORK CHICAGO SAN FRANCISCO ATHENS LONDON
MADRID MEXICO CITY MILAN NEW DELHI
SINGAPORE SYDNEY TORONTO

1 2 3 4 5 6 7 8 9   LCR   28 27 26 25 24 23

ISBN   978-1-265-22328-1
MHID   1-265-22328-9

e-ISBN   978-1-265-22379-3
e-MHID   1-265-22379-3

\

Library of Congress Cataloging-in-Publication Data

Names: Cadillac, Josh, author.
Title: Close for Life: the real estate agent's guide to creating satisfied customers that only do business with you / by Josh Cadillac.
Other titles: Close for life
Description: 1 Edition. | New York : McGraw Hill, [2023] | Includes bibliographical references and index.
Identifiers: LCCN 2023005544 (print) | LCCN 2023005545 (ebook) | ISBN 9781265223281 (hardback) | ISBN 9781265223793 (ebook)
Subjects: LCSH: Customer relations. | Selling—Customer services. | Real estate business.
Classification: LCC HF5415.5 .C33 2023 (print) | LCC HF5415.5 (ebook) | DDC 658.8/12—dc23/eng/20230517
LC record available at https://lccn.loc.gov/2023005544
LC ebook record available at https://lccn.loc.gov/2023005545

McGraw Hill books are available at special quantity discounts to use as premiums and sales promotions or for use in corporate training programs. To contact a representative, please visit the Contact Us pages at www.mhprofessional.com.

McGraw Hill is committed to making our products accessible to all learners. To learn more about the available support and accommodations we offer, please contact us at accessibility@mheducation.com. We also participate in the Access Text Network (www.accesstext.org), and ATN members may submit requests through ATN.

To my dad, who was a tough boss, great businessman,
and a guy who always found the time to teach me, and
to my mom, who held us all together and whose example
of generosity and kindness makes her one of
the most beautiful souls to ever grace this planet

CONTENTS

PART III
GET YOUR CUSTOMER RIGHT

PART IV
BUILD A BUSINESS YOU'RE PROUD OF

PREFACE

The real estate industry has a lot of issues, and these issues make people think some pretty not nice things when they find out you are an agent. It's not quite like finding out that you just got out of prison, but it's not like discovering you won the Nobel Prize either.

In addition to that, there is tremendous turnover in the industry from folks that either burn out or find out that they just can't take it. While some of these issues are specific to real estate, many of the biggest issues are endemic to society today. We live in a country that gives tremendous opportunities to us to be successful. We have a system that gives relative certainty that what is agreed to is what will happen. Then why is it that many people are frustrated and disenchanted with the work that they do and the amount of their life that work "steals" from what they actually love to do?

The Founding Fathers may have had it right when they wrote:

> We hold these truths to be self-evident, that all men are created equal, that they are endowed by their Creator with certain unalienable Rights, that among these are Life, Liberty and the Pursuit of a Paycheck.

Wait a minute . . . that doesn't sound quite right, does it? Hustling to lock down money for fast cars, parties in Vegas, and expensive wristwatches was definitely not what the Founding Fathers dreamed about in the Declaration of Independence. Yet that's what many Americans aspire to do today. The fast-paced consumer culture has infiltrated our collective mentality like a plague, and we have become focused on closing deals as quickly as possible to fund that lifestyle. This approach has real consequences.

When the founders described the pursuit of happiness, it wasn't the pursuit of immediate gratification; it was actually the joy one achieves from the pursuit of a life well lived. Wow, now that is a mouthful, huh?

A life well lived is taking a look at the really big picture. What do I mean by that? The big picture is keeping in mind what we are building toward each and every day, as opposed to what makes us feel good in the moment and then leaves us empty and chasing the next thing 10 minutes later. For many, modern culture has robbed them of that pursuit of happiness that is so inherently American. They don't have time or energy to appreciate the process of finding joy in a life well lived.

While it may sound counterintuitive, in regard to real estate, the reason that deals actually *don't* get closed is because customers feel used, unsatisfied, and misunderstood. But there's something we can do about it. We can start closing customers instead of deals.

One of the questions I always want answered is who the heck is talking, and why should I listen. So here goes.

I've been a top-selling real estate agent from the time I entered the industry. Even if a bunch of other agents are being interviewed to get a listing, I'm the one who walks out with the paperwork signed more than 90 percent of the time. I have more real estate certifications and designations than you can shake a stick at. My expertise, teaching method, and technique have earned me recognition as a national speaker and most recently as the Miami Association of Realtors Speaker of the Year. My material has been purchased and used as a requirement for post-license training for all agents in my area. I am author of the most state-approved continuing education courses in Florida, and I have created the first ever crypto and real estate class approved in the state as well as several others. Additionally, I run a real estate investment fund and a construction company, and I have built my own large and growing empire of investment properties.

Though I've had a great deal of success, my primary focus isn't on doing deals or closing transactions. Sounds a bit odd, right? My exceptional results aren't just because I am some kind of genius or happen to be way better looking than everyone else. (People think my English bulldog is better looking than I am. And they're right.) Instead, it's simply because I go in understanding what the customer is actually looking for in an agent:

- They want someone they like.
- They want someone who knows what the heck he or she is doing.
- And they want someone they trust to look out for them.

If I achieve those three things, I'll never have to waste money on advertising. The customers who work with me will never want to leave. That is what it means to Close for Life. Buyers are left with an experience they don't feel they can replicate anywhere else, and you become their go-to person for anything related to what you do. When you run your business that way, your work becomes something you're proud of, and it develops into an asset in your life.

I'll give you a short example.

I once took on a condo that was a $35,000 short sale. It was a lot of work for a fairly small payoff, but I treated it like I would any other deal. I worked with the customer to identify exactly what she needed to do, and I guided her through the process as a trusted advisor. By doing the deal well, I was able to get her $180,000 loan forgiven with her bank, and she walked out debt-free, and more importantly, as a very happy customer. Unbeknown to me, her son was looking to sell his $8 million house. Because I had done well by his mother, the son gave me that listing and several others thereafter. I had no idea that such a large series of transactions was waiting on the other side of the condo sale, but I treated the customer as if there were. Every customer deserves that kind of attention.

As I write this, we are grappling with an impending recession in the United States. If the economy turns sharply down, I'm sure the lazy people will look for excuses about why they're not able to succeed. They'll focus on external market factors and complain about how hard it is to stay afloat. Undoubtedly, their results will suffer as their customers hightail it away from them. After all, who wants to work with someone with a negative outlook?

But you? By reading this book you are setting yourself up to be different. If you apply what's here, you're going to focus on constantly striving to make *yourself* better. *Close for Life* will teach you what to do, and the result is that you and your business will become virtually recession-proof.

This book will help you take charge of your business, stop making excuses, and deeply understand what your customer needs and how your product can fit in. You'll become an indispensable member of your customer's team, and your customer will never seek to replace you or get tired of referring you to others.

Think about it through the lens of insurance sales. If you're talking to a guy and he's just trying his hardest to sell you a policy, unless you desperately want insurance, it's in one ear and out the other. You might sign on the dotted line just to get it over with, but you have no loyalty. If a different salesperson comes along and offers you something better, you probably will switch to that salesperson's company come renewal time.

Now, compare that to someone who genuinely tries to understand what you want to accomplish, the business you're in, and what sort of risk you're comfortable with. Then the person recommends products that are better suited to what you need than what you had been asking for. When he makes that professional recommendation on a policy and supports it with his own knowledge, he probably just went a long way toward earning your business for the rest of your life. This is the kind of result you want to achieve in your own work. And the great thing about this approach is that it makes the work that you do not just more helpful for the customer but also more meaningful for you.

No matter where you are in your career, this book will fundamentally change the way you do business.

One of the things that has always surprised me with the real estate classes I teach is that there will be people who have been in the business for 40 years seated right next to someone who is brand new to the industry. Both types of learners walk away happy because the things we talk about are incredibly important, and yet they are not commonly discussed in the real estate industry. The big picture is neglected, and the small picture fails to satisfy because it doesn't give us the direction and goals we need.

That is exactly what this book seeks to remedy. No longer will you be rushing to close deals so you can pay the bills. Instead, you're going to be selling a product that you understand and believe will provide value in the lives of your customers.

STEPHEN'S STORY

Let me tell you about Stephen. He was a young guy just starting out in a job selling radio advertising for a small local station. He really wanted to make the business work and was under a great deal of financial pressure to be successful. As he struggled to close deals, his bosses gave him advice that is very common in sales: Call more leads, come up with clever marketing pieces to help attract more clients, and keep pushing because "it's a numbers game." Stephen was frustrated, not making much money, and thinking of quitting. A mutual friend asked me to speak with him. I shared the Close for Life mindset.

The first thing I told him to do was ignore the terrible advice from his bosses. Getting more warm bodies through the door was not going to help; what he really needed to focus on was making prospective customers see that he knew what he was talking about and was looking out for their best interests.

Once he had initiated his mindset shift, Stephen's next assignment from me was to get the product knowledge to establish himself as well informed in the field. I told him to learn everything he could about his industry and never stop learning more. I prompted him to go to current and past customers and ask why they used the type of advertising they did, what their biggest concerns were, and what got them over those concerns. He had to understand what his product did well and what it didn't. I told him, "There is never an excuse to not be prepared to talk about the thing you sell for a living. If you can't do that, you are not a victim of circumstance. You are simply not prepared."

The third phase for Stephen was learning how to convey that he could be a valued member of the customer's team. For example, if the customer was looking for content creation, but Stephen got an inkling that cost might be a concern, he had to be able to provide the customer a great group of options at various price points. He had to be able to listen to the customer and understand at a deep level how his product could address the customer's needs, then lean on his product knowledge to explain it in a way that made sense to the customer. The goal was to show the customer that Stephen would be there as a trusted expert who would hold the customer's best interests above all else.

Stephen took these lessons to heart, and his interactions with customers radically changed. As he better understood his product and the power it had, he was able to transition from feeling like he was trying to "sell someone" to actually bringing something good into the customer's life. He became much more at ease in his interactions with clients, and new customers were drawn to him as they realized that his knowledge base was more comprehensive than that of other salespeople.

He also learned that his product was not necessarily right for every person, and he gained the confidence to be open and make referrals to other agencies with different offerings that would address the customer's needs. Stephen saw that the people he was honest with came back to him with different ideas or customer referrals. He's now the first person his customers think about when it comes to advertising. If there's ever a referral opportunity with someone in their network, they immediately say, "Oh, you've gotta talk to my guy."

Stephen is now the number one salesperson at his company. He has one of the highest conversion rates of anyone the station has ever employed. Most importantly, he loves to go to work every day.

It was important for me to coach Stephen on the importance of relentlessly pursuing excellence in his work because I believe that my own business is a reflection of me and the standards I have for my life. If I can look at the significant part of my life that is dedicated to work, I can proudly say that I'm not just doing what I do for the sake of a paycheck. My business is meaningful. It brings value to people and allows them to confidently make an informed decision to purchase the right real estate at the right time. Most people perceive work as somewhere you go that takes life away from you. My job *gives me* life. I want you to experience that joy of running a business well and having pride of ownership in what you do.

That is what *Close for Life* will give you.

INTRODUCTION

My Journey to Success in Real Estate

One of the most interesting things to ask people is how they got their start in the real estate industry. Some people respond that they were drawn to real estate as a career at an early age. Others fell into it in one way or another and found they liked it. Still others decided they needed a career change and selected real estate as a great field to make a new start.

While I had been involved in real estate for several years, my real start came after getting my butt kicked in the great recession of 2008. I was running the businesses my father had left me and managing the real estate holdings we had accumulated since he passed. We were in pretty decent shape we thought. Our properties were not highly leveraged. We were bringing to market a great restaurant concept. And we had built a team from folks that were proven performers in the industry.

Then 2008 happened. My restaurants—which had been growing well and on their way to being very profitable—suddenly fizzled as people stopped eating out. My real estate that was 100 percent occupied and had waiting lists of potential tenants fell to 65 percent occupancy, with many of the tenants falling behind on their rents. We quickly could not afford the mortgages anymore and lost one property after the other. The restaurants went under, too, as well as just about everything I owned, including the home I grew up in.

I had to start from scratch.

LESSONS FROM MY FATHER

All I really had were the lessons my father taught me and what I had picked up in my young business career to that point. While I greatly respected my father, I found myself wondering if his lessons were things that may have worked in a different time and didn't apply to the present situation. Maybe they were the ramblings of an old man who forgot what really made him succeed, or maybe he did well because of dumb luck and just attributed it to the things he told me about. When you're on the bottom looking for a way up, these are the kinds of things that go through your head, not to mention the fear, guilt, and frustration you feel as you struggle with just how unfair this whole thing is.

Over time, as I pulled myself up, I came to realize that my father's lessons still worked. They became the foundation of how I conduct my business, and I continue to use them to this day.

By the time I came along, my dad, Bob Cadillac, was an older guy and almost completely retired. He had lived a full and exceptionally interesting life. As just one example of his crazy brilliance and killer instinct, he had paid $250,000 in the 1950s for the second computer IBM ever made. He had patents out the wazoo. He once convinced Motorola to come down to his plant and figure out cell phones before anyone had thought of it because he needed to stay in touch with his drivers.

He spent a lot of time with me growing up, and I benefited immensely from his life lessons and the values he instilled. He had been in military school and the army, and he did a great job of putting me in positions where I had to do hard things that he knew would frustrate me but would help me to discover what I was truly capable of.

My dad had a restaurant business. He started bringing food to students in the local church school I was attending. It began as a charity, but it eventually morphed into an actual business with a contract in place.

My dad thought it would be a good idea if I became one of his employees to learn the value of hard work. From the time I was about nine years old, I worked from 6:00 in the morning until 1:00 in the afternoon in the school cafeteria we ran, and then I was homeschooled for the rest of the day.

At first, I was not what you would call a model employee. I was a lazy, lazy little kid. Seeing this, Dad decided that I needed some motivational supervision, so he got one of his former foremen from New York to be my boss. He was a former Marine who had been notorious for being one of the toughest guys in my father's industrial operation. By the time he started working with me, he was crippled with arthritis and tasked solely with making sure I did what I was supposed to do. Let me tell you, he rode me like a rented mule for about two years.

Eventually, one of the main people in the business left, and I could see that my mom was about to have a lot dumped on her plate. Maybe it was because I had been beaten down by my boss for so long, or perhaps it was just a product of getting older, but this is when I really stepped up. I stopped being a problem and started to really contribute to the business. I learned to start being the "stand-up guy" who did what was needed when it was needed that my dad always wanted me to be. So, when my father passed away in 2002, the natural thing was to step up and do what he left that needed doing. That meant growing the business.

By 2008, I had several property holdings, including a large office building and multibay warehouse industrial operation. I also still had my dad's cafeteria business, and I was leveraging our position with the properties to fund two new restaurants.

AFTER THE CRASH

While the real estate collapse was not my fault, I certainly participated in the fallout in a very meaningful way. I felt like I let people close to me down and was wracked with guilt.

My mother and to a lesser extent my siblings looked to me to come up with a solution. I was in charge, and this happened on my watch. I couldn't fall into the trap of feeling sorry for myself, which I had seen paralyze so many folks. I knew I had to do something to steer us in a new direction.

The most obvious option was real estate. I had been around real estate from the time I was three or four years old, when I would go to meetings in Manhattan with my dad and listen to him talk business for hours. It was something that was always part of my family's history, so I thought that would be a good fit for a path to build back what I had lost.

But while real estate looked attractive, I had a major concern. One major lesson I had learned from my dad was a serious sense of responsibility. He told me to never take on a commitment if I didn't know I could complete it. This was especially true when it came to doing transactions that could risk someone else's money. I had to know what I was doing.

I realized that while I understood real estate as a landlord, I didn't know everything I needed to know to be an active real estate agent. I needed to quickly bridge my knowledge gap. So, after I got my real estate license, I took every real estate course that I could find. This was not just multiple listing service (MLS) trainings, but also pretty much every single major professional certification or designation course offered in the field. I traveled to other states when I couldn't find the classes I wanted locally. I partnered with seasoned agents and my broker to make sure I learned every aspect of the job, and, most importantly, so I didn't make any mistakes that hurt a customer.

I committed to learning everything I could. I pursued education with the goal of being able to answer anything a customer could possibly throw at me. To develop a competitive advantage, I took multiple licensing exams: real estate, general contractor, and mortgage.

As I accessed a variety of educational resources (books, blog posts, classes, etc.), I realized many didn't feel like a high-quality use of my time. The content just wasn't all that good. Still, I persisted in growing my knowledge so that I could help my customers and develop my career.

I began working for a local brokerage in the mornings prior to the restaurant opening. I eventually teamed up with a very nice gentleman and friend who was highly skilled at bringing in deals. He would bring in the lead, and I did my best to handle the rest. I became an expert in short sales and had more active listings than just about anyone else in the state: 70–80 at a time. Most agents would have been happy closing 15 percent of them. *I closed 95 percent.*

At some point, the knowledge that I picked up doing short sales gave me insider access to a lot of distressed assets. I started pulling together investors, doing the analysis for them, and getting them into great investments.

I parlayed that knowledge, with my business partner, into the acquisition of nonperforming mortgages. I bought mortgages already in default at significant discounts to the market value. That drew the eye of other investors, who would put up 100 percent of the purchase capital while I covered the renovations and legal fees. Once the property was fixed up and sold, we'd each recover our costs and then split the profits equally.

My ability to attract those investors and execute on the deals came simply from the vast product knowledge I had built over time. Most agents would have had no clue how to do this and no desire to learn. They might have just gone the traditional route of buying and flipping houses retail. Had I followed suit, I wouldn't have made a tenth of the profit I actually did.

TEACHING REAL ESTATE

By that point, I was enough of an industry standout that people began telling me that I should teach classes. I was at a national brokerage, and I had earned the reputation of being able to handle even the most complicated or unusual deals. I started with just helping other agents, but eventually I caught the eye of the local association, and the folks there suggested that I write a class. I developed an initial two-day course that ran the gamut from email signature to differential cash flow, negotiation, contracts, and everything in between.

The first time I delivered it was in Pensacola, Florida. Afterward, a gentleman who had been in the business for 35 years walked up to me and said that no one had ever explained real estate investing as clearly as I had. That's when I knew that I had something worth really pursuing. Being able to distill information and drive a high return on agents' investment of time, for both new entrants to the industry and decades-long veterans like that man, was something the industry desperately needed, and I now knew what I wanted to do.

Over the past fourteen years, I've taught hundreds of classes for tens of thousands of students. The agents that I trained and who implemented what I teach have experienced disproportional success. And the ones who didn't? Nearly all of them have left the industry.

WHY I WROTE THIS BOOK

The thing I realized through my educational pursuits was that what I learned in classes didn't really prepare me for the job of being a real estate agent at all. In fact, the classes completely neglected what I eventually learned were the keys to achieving success in this industry.

After all the courses, books, and research, I sensed something was missing. The lessons from my father continued to resonate in the back of my mind. I began to experiment with applying those lessons in my real estate work. Over time, the application of those lessons fundamentally changed not just how I work, but why I work the way that I do. In short, I learned how to get the best out of myself and how to connect with and help my customers.

There are three fundamental things that I realized are either neglected or gotten flat-out wrong in real estate.

The first thing is that we often get ourselves wrong as individuals in this business. Most agents are taught to quickly close as many deals as possible. That's wrong. We should instead focus on making prospective customers see that we know what we're talking about and that we are looking out for our customers' best interests.

The second thing we often don't develop is our product knowledge. Too many agents pretty much stop learning after getting their license. Real estate is a complex and multifaceted industry. There's no excuse to stop learning.

The third thing is that we often don't take the time to deeply understand our customers. We must listen better. Customers' real estate needs and financial situations change over time. We should strive to become a trusted and valuable advisor to our customers so that they will turn to us for help throughout their lives and careers.

I've organized this book to address these three areas. Part I, "Get Yourself Right," discusses the principles and mental approach that are the foundation of success in real estate. Part II, "Get Your Product

Right," explains the importance of knowing your product and understanding the economic fundamentals of the industry. Part III, "Get Your Customer Right," shows how to build rapport and establish credibility with your customers. And rounding out the book, there is a Part IV, "Build a Business You're Proud of." It is a reminder of what is essential in life—that being true to your customers and to yourself matters deeply.

Let's get started.

PART I

GET YOURSELF
RIGHT

CHAPTER 1

YOU'RE THE CEO

When it comes to being a real estate agent or broker, we have a couple of pieces of good news along with one piece of bad news. That's a 2-to-1 good-to-bad ratio, which is a lot better than the 50-50 deal we get with most jobs, so that's promising.

The first piece of good news is that you are your own company. We will call it You LLC. Congratulations!

The second piece of good news: Guess who the CEO of You LLC is? It's you! Congratulations. You are the boss, head honcho, the big kahuna, el chazo grande.

Here's the promised bad news though. Guess who the staff of You LLC is? It is also you. Especially when you're just starting out in this business, you're the one that has to answer the phones, file the paperwork, and handle the bazillions of things that must get done. The issue starts when doing these tasks blinds us to the fact that we're also responsible for running our company.

THE STAFF HAT

There are a tremendous number of tasks to do in our business. If you look around at the industry, you'll see that most agents are stuck with their staff hat on their entire time at work. Ask yourself, what tasks do you devote most of your time to? Is it the type of task that if you got busy enough, you could hire someone else to do? Activities like showing property, making marketing pieces, searching the MLS, generating leads, etc., all fall under the heading of staff tasks. Sure, those tasks are all important and need to get done. The problem is, those staff tasks are so time consuming that most agents never bother to find the time to put on their CEO hat.

It's tough being the CEO and the staff at the same time. I'm sure you know people who try to do both in their jobs and maybe their personal lives too. Taken to an extreme, trying to do everything perfectly contributes to the schizophrenia that is the human existence.

The CEO cares about the future and is concerned with your long-term well-being. The CEO is willing to delay gratification now so you can have something better in the future. The CEO wants you to do well in the future and experience long-term wins.

On the other hand, the staff wants pleasure, and it wants it now. It doesn't care about the future. It will figure that out when it gets here. An example of this mentality can be seen in the highly philosophical show *The Simpsons*. Marge tells Homer that one day his kids will be all grown up and leave the house and he will regret not spending more time with them. Homer responds that this is a problem for future Homer and he sure doesn't envy that guy, while he simultaneously mixes a bunch of vodka with a jar of mayonnaise and proceeds to drink it. *Spoiler alert:* Future Homer passed out.

This silly example shows us something we do all the time, though usually to a lesser extent. Who here has ever had an argument or negotiation with yourself? My arguments with myself usually center on the consumption of baked confections. It goes something like this: A little voice in my head says, "You know I think I saw a package of double-stuffed Oreos in the pantry. You like double-stuffed Oreos." Then the CEO chimes in and says, "It isn't cheat day. You aren't supposed to eat sweets until the weekend. Have you seen how many calories are in those things. How do they even fit them all? You don't want to toss away all the work you've been doing in the gym, do you?" At which point the staff chimes in with something along the lines of, "Exactly, you have been working so hard in the gym, and you are just going to have one (which we all know is humanly impossible). You'll do extra cardio tomorrow."

Does that argument sound familiar? Maybe your argument is about getting up in the morning earlier, reading more, watching less TV, or going to the gym. This CEO-staff conflict goes on whenever we don't have direct supervision, as in the case with our life. The reason I've highlighted this in Chapter 1 is because we have so little supervision in real estate. We don't have a boss. We have a broker. We are not the broker's employees though; we are independent contractors. This means when we said we will be in the office at 9 a.m. and don't show till 9:45, our broker will not be there with a baseball bat saying something like, "You're late. Where have you been?" This means that if we don't hold ourselves to standards, then there isn't anyone to do it for us. It brings up a several important questions:

- Is your CEO or your staff running your company?
- How good is your CEO at getting your staff to do what the CEO knows the staff needs to do?
- How much of your time at work do you spend on staff tasks, such as:
  - Showing properties
  - Creating marketing pieces
  - Searching listings
  - Others

- How much time do you spend on CEO actions?
  - Setting up systems to help your staff to be more productive
  - Managing your morale
  - Holding yourself accountable
  - Others

MY SUIT GUY

The evidence for this CEO-staff issue is most clearly seen, for my money, when I ask agents all over the country that I teach, "How would you define 'closing'?" The answers I get are typically along the lines of, "It is finally over," "the finish line," "payday," "cha-ching," or some similar variant. The problem with these answers is that they clearly show who is running their company—and it's not the CEO.

If you ask employees why they work, they will usually say something like, "Because they are paying me," or "To pay for____," or "I'm working for the weekend." To be clear, that is a paycheck or a finish line that is exactly like the answers the agents gave me for their definition of closing. In real estate, agents' staffs overwhelmingly run their companies, and the customer is the loser for it.

Why does the CEO of a company work? Well, sometimes the CEO takes reduced pay, or even no pay. In fact, some CEOs will take money out of their pocket to put into their business. So, in these cases, the CEOs are not working for the paycheck. There doesn't seem to be a finish line for them either, at least one that can be easily seen. These CEOs are not trying to get paid today; they are instead trying to build a business that pays them for the rest of their life.

The best way to build a strong business is to develop a loyal base of customers that would never think of doing business with anyone else. The alternative is what mainstream real estate teaches: more leads, more scripts, more ways to manipulate customers into using us so that we can get paid today. You see, the CEO doesn't want to close deals. The CEO wants to close customers for life.

Let me tell you about my suit guy. Really, he was my dad's suit guy that I sort of inherited. My dad was Italian and a successful businessman from New York, and basically the rule in his day was that you had to have a suit guy. The suit guy would make suits for my dad, and later on when I came around, he would make an identical small suit for me so my dad and I would match.

I am a fan of old movies, and one day I was watching *Casablanca*. In that movie, Humphrey Bogart wears this beautiful, white, double-breasted tuxedo. I see this tuxedo and think to myself, that is a great outfit, and it makes Bogie look so cool. I am not nearly as cool as he is, but maybe if I had a tuxedo like that, I might fool people into thinking I am.

Armed with this incredible logical train wreck, I decide to see my suit guy. I say to him, "Hey, Giuseppe (yep, that's his name), how are you doing?" He says, "Hey, Josh, I'm doing great."

I tell him, "My friend, last night I watched *Casablanca*, and in that movie, Bogie is wearing a . . ." He immediately interrupts me and says, "The white double-breasted tuxedo." I say yes, and he responds, "That is a gorgeous suit and iconic piece of clothing."

I tell him that I agree, and I ask him if he can get me suit like that. He says, "Geez, Josh, I could do it, but that tuxedo isn't made anymore. It would need to be a special order, and it would be very expensive. As beautiful as that tuxedo is, it's not really the style anymore. More than that, Josh, double-breasted suits are made for guys who are tall and skinny, and frankly you don't check either of those boxes. I think you'd be happier with something like this." He then proceeds to show me a catalog with a tuxedo that would cost significantly less.

This story shows why my suit guy is my suit guy. He is the clothing professional in the room. He listened to what I wanted and didn't just try to sell me a suit. He actually made a lot less than he could have selling me the more expensive suit. But he doesn't want to sell me a suit. He wants to sell me every suit I am ever going to own, and his choice to forgo a paycheck and his desire to do what is best for me is exactly what entitles him to that business. This is why I will jump on a plane and fly past thousands of other possible suit acquisition locations to see my suit guy.

FIND YOUR CEO VOICE

That CEO gig is a hard and thankless job in a lot of ways. It forces us to have and maintain standards for how we do business. Because no one is looking over our shoulders, it is easy to let your standards deteriorate. In doing so, you might be tempted to do whatever you can to make it easier for yourself as the staff member. But is that really what's best for your company?

To become a true CEO, you really have to take a step back and say, "Wait a second. Let me not act like the things I'm putting in place are going to be my responsibility. Let me put my CEO hat on and think about what the best thing would be to build a business. What kind of business do I want to run? What do I want to be known for? What does the company need? Why am I doing this business? What is the goal? What does success look like?" And a question that often weighs heavily on my CEO's mind, "What do you want people saying about you when your time here is done." These are the questions you need to be asking yourself (the CEO), without you (the staff) present.

I know that sounds a little nuts, but it's important to divorce yourself from thinking about being the one that will have to do the work that needs to be done and instead simply ask the questions: "What does my business need to get done to achieve the goals and standards I have set? What resources do I have available to me to get this done? What can I reasonably expect to get from my staff, and how can I motivate my staff to get the most out of them?"

One of the big areas where agents screw up is right there. Either they are too hard and critical with themselves—which often makes them timid, controlling, or paralyzed because they feel they must be perfect. Or the other alternative is they are too soft on themselves and thus are constantly excusing away their shortcomings—they are lazy, and as a result, they will never achieve what they are capable of.

We have to learn to be a good boss to ourselves. This means our CEO has to look at the staff as the chief piece of production equipment in the business. A good boss learns how to get the best out of the employees. The goal is to help the employees achieve more than they could on their own. This means often pushing the staff beyond what they thought they were capable of doing.

A good boss lays out what needs to be done and holds the staff accountable for those expectations. Having challenging but reasonable expectations is the key. We want to develop our staff to be the best they can be. We want to understand what we do well and what we don't do well. We can improve ourselves by introducing systems that help us to do the things we suck at and hate to do (as a CEO should). We need to go into the process of developing ourselves like a boss that genuinely wants to maximize our potential and help us to be as happy and successful as we can be.

There is a famous story about an interview with Andrew Carnegie that highlights the idea of how a good boss is able to successfully develop people and therefore how your CEO should work to develop your staff. A reporter asked Mr. Carnegie how he had managed to hire 43 millionaires. Carnegie told the reporter that those men had not been millionaires when they came to work for him but had become so as a result of working for him. The reporter then asked him how he was able to develop these men so that they became valuable enough to be paid such high salaries. Carnegie's response was, "Men are developed the same way gold is mined. When gold is mined, several tons of dirt must be moved to get an ounce of gold, but one doesn't go into the mine looking for dirt—one goes in looking for the gold."

We all have an inner CEO voice that is unique to us. This means your inner voice will sound different from mine. My inner CEO voice sometimes sounds a lot like my first boss, Sam, a retired Marine, who was super hard on me as a kid. If I have something to finish on a Saturday morning, but I am being lazy, my inner voice says, "Get your ass out of bed you, lazy sack of . . . You know what needs to get done."

Our CEO voice is the one that holds us accountable. Our staff voice just wants to have a good time now. Our inner voice though is a tool of the CEO. The one critical question you need to ask is if your inner voice is the best one to help you to develop, or does it just sound like a critical person from your past and get in the way of you getting the most out of yourself. That retired Marine's voice works well for my CEO, and so I use it. If it needed to sound more like Stuart Smalley, Mickey Mouse, or Florence Nightingale to get more out of me, then that is what I would need to change it to. Keep the goal in mind: There is a better version of me in me, and I want to get it out and make it shine.

I talk a lot about pushing because, let's be honest, most of us don't push hard enough. We should push with excellence. Balance and rest are important, though. One of the best things to keep in mind is, "The opposite of one type of crazy is still crazy." The opposite of being a lazy layabout is being obsessed with work. Neither of these is healthy nor is in line with the pursuit of happiness. For this reason, sometimes my inner voice is a little softer, and I have to figure out who's talking. Maybe one day I'm really feeling tired and don't have the energy to get to the gym. My staff voice might say, "Great, take the day off and go eat some Oreo cookies!" My CEO voice might also agree to take the day off, but only because I've genuinely been pushing myself too hard and need to look out for my long-term health.

Learning to differentiate between our inner CEO and staff voice is critical to starting to win the battles with ourselves. If we are going to push hard with excellence, then we are also going to need to learn to commit to rest the same way, because life is too short to pursue the important things with mediocrity.

The thing to realize is our successes and failures define us to ourselves. If you are a person that goes to the gym regularly, you know that about yourself; and when you say you are going to go, you believe that you are the type of person that fulfills that commitment. If you are a person that has been promising for years that you will do different things and hasn't, then you are the type of person that doesn't keep promises to yourself. You lie to yourself, and you have made that OK. It is not OK. Setting the precedent that lying to yourself is completely unacceptable is very important to have the self-respect necessary to run a successful business and accomplish what you set out to do.

The main benefits of building the type of business that closes for life is that it immediately differentiates you from your competitors that are just trying to get paid. The other benefit is that it makes you maintain standards that are higher than what the industry would accept and what you know you could get away with. This builds into the self-respect we just discussed above. You define yourself as the kind of person that sets and holds to standards for your business because you are delivering a quality product. You know that what you bring to market for your customers is far better than what they could get elsewhere because of the sheer act of will of making it so by your efforts. You could do less and still succeed. By doing this you get the pride of knowing you give your customers a true quality product. You could choose to be Casio (heck, the company sells a lot of watches), but there is a lot more pride put into the product Rolex puts out.

A story I heard a long time ago that always stuck with me on this was about a farmer that had done really well for himself and decided that instead of driving around to inspect his fields in his old pickup, he would treat himself to an upgrade. He decided to buy himself a Rolls-Royce. He loved his new car and the way he felt driving around and inspecting all he had built. One day though as he was driving, he noticed something in one of his fields that caught his eye, and it distracted him just enough that he swerved and ran over a big rock, which broke the axle on his car.

He went and got a couple of horses and towed the car into the barn, and then placed a call to the service department for Rolls-Royce and told the folks there what happened. They told him they did not have a local service department but that they would figure out how to resolve the issue for him. A couple of days later, a helicopter showed up with a new axle and four Rolls-Royce technicians to install it. They fixed the car and left, taking off the same way they arrived. The farmer's immediate thought was, "Holy crap, this is going to be the most expensive auto repair ever!"

He started anticipating and dreading the bill that he knew would be coming. Every day he went out and checked the mail but still no bill. He waited months, but the bill never came. Finally, it was nearing the end of the year, and he was upset. He called up the billing department of Rolls-Royce and explained the situation. The person at the other end of the line told him to hold as he needed to transfer him to the service director. The service director picked up, and the farmer once again explained the situation and finished with, "This has been pending for months, and I am closing out my year now. If I don't get this bill soon, I am not going to pay it."

To this the head of service replied, "Sir, the axles on Rolls-Royces don't break. Have a nice day, sir."

There was no bill because the company has standards. If something goes wrong, Rolls-Royce fixes it. There is a reason the reputation of some automakers is different than that of others. You can choose to be a Yugo or a Rolls-Royce. The standards you set in your business are what will or will not differentiate you from all the other options out there the customer has to choose from.

You are the CEO. You get to decide. Will you be a Rolls-Royce or just some cheap, gray, mass-produced car people can't tell apart until they see the name badge. Your company. Your standards. You get the credit when they are met, and you bear the responsibility when they aren't. You have the power—but with it you must accept the responsibility to build your business into one you can be proud of and build yourself into the type of person that pursues the joy of a life well lived in all you do. Life's too short to pursue anything less than excellence.

STANDARDS TO LIVE BY

Here are some standards I implemented in my business that allowed me to experience the success I did so quickly. I didn't always do these perfectly, but this is what my company strove to be and what my CEO sought to implement.

- My company is respectful of people's time—which means I am on time. If I am ever late for some reason, I apologize genuinely and let the person know why and that this is not how I run my business.
- My company answers the phone. If I miss a call, I return it immediately and apologize for missing the call and tell the person why the call was missed.
- My company answers emails immediately. If I can't fully answer the content of the email's request, I immediately acknowledge receipt and let the sender know when I should be able to do so.
- My company does what it says. I strive to be so consistent that I am taken for granted. I want people to get the best night's sleep of their life when they give me something because they know it will be done. This means I show up and I don't let

people down.

- My company knows its product well. More to come on this in future chapters, but suffice it to say, I know what I sell, why it is a good thing, how it works, and how it helps my customers.
- My company fights for our customers. I am committed to negotiate the best deal possible for my customers even if they are willing to take less. I will always try to get my customers the best deal I can if given the opportunity.
- My company does everything with excellence. Not perfection.
- My company will always be learning. It is OK to say "I don't know" to something once, but I will never say "I don't know" to the same thing twice. I will build in and improve my capacity to be the best version of me I can be.
- My company will expect and endure through hard times. When it gets hard, I will dig in and push harder. My CEO will find ways to keep my staff (me) driven and motivated through the hard times, as he knows employee morale is his responsibility.
- My company will always tell my customers what is best for them regardless of what is best for me.
- My company will be accountable. I will admit my mistakes and accept responsibility. I won't lie to others, and I won't lie to me.
- My company does the right thing. I run my business with integrity.
- My company puts the customer first in communication. I will constantly look for better ways to explain things, and I will have empathy for my listeners.
- My company is constantly improving. I get stuff done, and I compete with myself to get things completed faster than the deadline and more quickly than what people thought was possible.
- My company is grateful. What I have is the result of many other people's generosity and the kindness of sharing their wisdom. I will do my best to be accepting of other people's short-

comings and to be humble about my successes.

I put "my company" in the standards above, but read them again and substitute "I" instead to make them more personal to you.

The list above sets out business standards I have for me. I didn't actively make this list, but instead it is a collection of the things I learned from the people I did business with and respected and from my father's examples. Looking back to where my success came from, I can see that this mindset was the starting point to clearly differentiate myself from my competitors and gave me the edge in building a loyal customer base that would never work with anyone else ever. The thing that's crazy is that none of these things were part of any real estate class I ever took.

These standards are the heart of "the pursuit" part of "the pursuit of happiness" from the Declaration of Independence.

Over the years, your list of standards should change and adapt to get the most out of you and your business. As I pursued new business opportunities and growth, I added new standards or highlighted things that should have been standards but weren't. Here are just a few examples for me that got added to my standards as I learned and adapted my business:

- My company is loyal to business associates and friends. I want loyal customers, and so I try to be one. I don't hop from brokerage to brokerage either.
- I set a good example for the people that work for me, and in turn my employees set a good example. I always worked hard, but now I make sure to do it in a way that helps my employees not to have excuses to not do work they can be proud of. This includes how I speak about customers with them and how they see me interact with those customers. Following my lead, my longer-term employees set a great example for the newer ones we bring on.

- My company only turns out a quality product. I will only write or teach a class I believe is excellent.
- My company fulfills our commitments. I make sure my partners make money.

The newest addition to this list (proof that we are implementing our commitment to always learning) is a mindset gift from some very generous friends (Jeff Wright, Mike Dandurand, and belatedly my dad):

- My company is always open to new opportunities: I say yes whenever possible.

WHAT ARE YOUR STANDARDS?

As CEO of You LLC, list the standards that your company should adhere to. Use these questions to help guide you:

- What does a business you can be proud of look like?
- What type of standards do you need to have to create that kind of business?
- What type of standards do people you admire in business have that you should adopt? How will you hold yourself accountable to these standards?
- How will you communicate these standards to others?

So, here's a quick example of how these standards look in practice: I was booked to speak in Chattanooga, Tennessee, and was flying from Fort Lauderdale. I had to teach from my office via Zoom all day, so I had to take the latest flight out the airline had that night. My flight had a stop and plane change in Atlanta. My first flight went perfectly, but things started to unravel for my second flight. I was supposed to leave at around 10 p.m., but when I got to the gate, I found out it was delayed. Then just after 11 p.m., the airline ticket agent told us the flight was canceled. The new flight would not leave till 7:35 a.m. I did some quick math and realized that even if everything went perfectly, that flight would make me late for the class the next day. (This is where the standards kicked in. I never considered being late or canceling.)

I needed to figure out how to get to Chattanooga that night. I immediately started work on getting a rental car and getting my bags off the plane. I was only 50 percent successful. I was told that the bags would take at least two hours to get off the plane and might not be available till tomorrow morning. So, no clothes or toothbrush for the next day. I did, however, secure a car and made the drive, arriving just after 2 a.m. Got to bed by 3 a.m. after seeing if there was a Walmart that I could go to the next morning to buy a dress shirt and some slacks to make sure I was dressed as my customers have come to expect.

I got four hours of sleep, but showed up and taught two of the best classes I have ever taught, because there is one more personal standard I didn't mention, and it's an important one: I live for a challenge. When it gets hard, I know it is a chance to redefine myself to myself as the kind of person that finds a way to make it through. I now know that if I have to give a full day of high-energy classes on very little sleep, I can do it—because I have done it before. The mystery and uncertainty are gone. If I did it in the past, I can do it again. There may be many hard situations that come up, but having overcome this challenge, other challenges don't seem so bad by comparison. My capacity has increased. I now know that, and no one can take that from me.

The folks that booked me for the speech were shocked when they heard the story of my mini odyssey to get there along with the positive feedback from the folks that took my classes. Their appreciation for the way I do my business resulted in a conversation on how we could do more work together. That wouldn't have happened if I took the very obvious excuse of "circumstances beyond my control" and didn't show up. That opportunity to get more business and work toward closing a customer for life was manufactured by just following my standards and finding a way to show up.

The really interesting part is that I didn't have to think about *if* I was going to get it done, because I had been working to build and internalize my standards to allow me to be a successful CEO to my staff. Standards that you set for your business allow your CEO to do the job, which will empower you to build yourself into the type of agent that delivers a great service that customers never want to replace.

CHAPTER 2

ARE YOU A SALESPERSON OR A CLOSER FOR LIFE?

One day I decided to go to Best Buy to get a new TV. As I entered the store, I had the same experience most of us have had in similar situations. Someone in a Best Buy shirt asked me as I entered if I needed any help, and I said no. This was an automatic reaction, and I didn't really think too much about it. That is until I got to the TV section and found four that were the right size with vastly different prices and specifications.

I then went looking all over the place to try to find a salesperson to help me. The reality is that when I went into the door of Best Buy, I did need help. Then why did I say no? I asked myself that while I was waiting to pay. Maybe I am weird? But as I watched while I waited, I saw several people do the same thing I did.

I soon realized that the reason for this response is because sales-people approach people constantly in one way or another. This has conditioned people to have an automatic "no" built in before they even get a chance to get going. Be honest. Do you listen to every telemarketer that calls, or do you look for the first chance to hang up?

For this reason, we need to try to sound as little like a salesperson as we can. People hate being sold to. In real estate, the extreme focus on lead generation, cold calling, drip campaigns, and guerrilla marketing exacerbates the issue of agents having to make a very uncomfortable and "salesy"-sounding pitch.

Many agents make matters worse by a lack of product knowledge (this is a problem we address more in a later chapter), which limits their ability to speak intelligently about issues people are interested in and once again leaves them sounding like a salesperson—all of which sets off our customers' preprogrammed "you're being sold to" response. The result is akin to how people would have behaved 500 years ago if they found out the person they were talking to had leprosy.

In addition to not liking salespeople in general, most customers have a perception problem specific to real estate salespeople. It's not as bad as finding out you are a convicted felon, but it's a lot closer to that than most agents realize. Customers typically do not think real estate agents are market experts. When people rank the credibility of various jobs, real estate agents usually come in just slightly better than used car salespeople and worse than attorneys.

This is what the customers think about agents before they meet them:

- They're lazy.
- They're overpaid.
- They're not very smart.
- They're all about the commission.

You may be offended by this and object, "How can they judge me like that. Judging people is wrong." Well, the fact is, everyone judges, no matter how politically correct a person claims to be. It is how the human brain works, and it does so to protect us based on what we have learned from our experiences in life.

Imagine you needed a last-minute babysitter for something you had to do. What would be the first three places you would check:

1. The biker bar on the corner?
2. The local parole officer to see if there are any parolees that might need some extra spending money?
3. The sex offender database?

Why not? You do realize you are judging all those people, don't you? You've never even walked a mile in their shoes. Society tells you that somehow judging them makes *us* bad people. That tends to dilute the idea that people judge us. It does so by making the people doing the judging into morally bad people for doing the judging and therefore their opinion doesn't matter. In other words, who cares what a bad person thinks? Unfortunately, that very logic is predicated on our judgment of them for having their opinion. Don't you just love it when arguments refute themselves?

Here is a fact: Your customers judge you, and they should. That doesn't make them bad people; it makes them smart and cautious. They have a right to vet the people they choose to work with (as would you) and to set the parameters by which they do that. If you don't consider that you are being judged by your customers, it makes you self-absorbed, unempathetic, and uninterested in actually helping people. Talk about some judging, huh?

HOW CUSTOMERS SEE US

Doing away with the excuse that people shouldn't judge allows us as agents to turn a critical eye on ourselves and to really consider how our customers see us. This allows us to make progress in being perceived by our customers in the most positive way possible.

By getting rid of the idea that if our customers don't like us, the problem is them, we're left a clear view of where the problem lies—with us. If customers don't like you, it's on you. So, lines like "If they don't like me, then that's on them" need to go.

Of course, you can't change other people's prejudgments of you. If you're an agent or a salesperson, you're being judged by the nature of the job you have. That is your problem to fix—not your customers'.

Think about it: Is the customer wrong to think poorly of real estate agents? Out of 1,000 randomly selected agents, how many agents would you say answer their phone? If you have a bit of experience in real estate, you know the answer. Not many.

It is almost a running joke in the industry that so many agents take pride in saying, "Oh, I only text." Well, that might be great for you, but maybe you should consider what customers think of that?

The Realtor Code of Ethics requires agents to use their best efforts to help their customers. Does that jibe with not answering phone calls? No, of course not, and that means the vast majority of agents are in breach of their own code of ethics—which are only supposed to be the minimum standard for business. That's another reason to set higher standards, as we discussed in the previous chapter.

How do we fix this perception among customers? It starts by realizing that we are in a well. Our customers have a very negative default opinion of us when we meet them, and we need to extricate ourselves as soon as possible if we are to have any hope of closing a customer for life.

The way out of the hole starts with not letting the customers confuse us with the other agents out there. If I run my business in a different way, I need to figure out how to manifest that in everything that I do.

There is a famous Bugs Bunny and Daffy Duck cartoon where they each keep changing the signs for duck and rabbit hunting season back and forth and then dressing up as the other one to not get shot. We don't want to disguise ourselves as an average agent. It is average agent hunting season, and I don't want to get shot by mistake. So, I don't want to sound or act like an average agent.

If I don't establish my credibility right away and the customers continue to view me in a negative light because they think poorly of all agents, there will be negative consequences that manifest themselves throughout the relationship. The most obvious ones are:

- **Customers won't tell you the truth.** If you were going to buy a used car, would you tell the salesperson how much money you planned to spend, or would you give the salesperson a lower number? Why wouldn't you tell the real number? Because you know the salesperson will find a way to spend all of it. If the customers think of you as a salesperson, then don't be surprised when they're not completely honest. They feel like you are going to use what they say against them and for your benefit.

- **Customers will question everything you suggest.** If you are out for you, then the customers will think your advice is in the interest of getting your commission and not necessarily in their best interests. They think of you as a mercenary, so they don't believe your interests are intertwined with theirs.

- **Customers will try to reduce your commission.** If you are not looking out for them, then they need to look out for themselves. They figure if you are going to get your pound of flesh from them by looking out for yourself first and getting them to spend too much, then they might as well get as much back as they can by cutting your pay. Besides, how much is a mercenary really worth?

WHO DO YOU WANT TO BE?

When you come in and hit the prospective customer with a line like, "Are you or anyone you know thinking of buying a house?," you play right into an unflattering profile. Right away, you establish yourself as someone with a transactional mindset who is only concerned with closing a deal as quickly as possible and then moving on to the next one. But is that really the kind of business that you want to run?

At the core, my Close for Life method starts with establishing a mindset to guide you in all your customer interactions. It starts with thinking about who you want to be in your business. Is it a person who just does the bare minimum to get a house sold and then moves on, chasing the next commission? Or is it someone who anticipates the customers' needs, demonstrates deep knowledge of the market, and proves to the customers that their best interests are front and center? I know who I'd rather be.

Rather than starting with trying to get the customers to sell, rent, or buy a property, my method starts with trying to turn the customers into the best buyer, seller, landlord, or tenant they can be. I want to give to them, not take. But for this to work, it's essential that the mindset is true and genuine. If it is not organic, it comes off as just more sales techniques—and one of the sleaziest kinds.

So, how do I do this? Here's a great example.

On the way into a listing presentation, I tell myself I don't want the listing; I just want to make sure these folks know how this works. I want to make sure that I provide them with enough information so that a less reputable agent will not be able to take advantage of them, and that they understand all their available options before I leave.

If they choose to reward me with their business, that is awesome; if not, that's OK too. Using this method, I secure more than 90 percent of the listings where I have an appointment.

My approach starts with caring about the customer more than you care about your commission. One of the lines I love is, "People don't care how much you know until they know how much you care."

When was the last time you got a phone call from someone who sold you a product? Can you even remember? Has it *ever* happened? But think about how you would feel if your real estate agent (or car salesperson, Apple Genius Bar expert, or Louis Vuitton associate) called you up six months after your purchase just to genuinely ask how things were going with the product?

Your initial reaction probably would be confusion when you realized the caller wasn't trying to sell you something. After that, you likely felt surprised. Would that kind of check-in call make the person stand out from other people you have purchased something from? What if those calls kept coming every few months for years? Would you consider the amount of time and commitment it must take to call? Would you start to feel like you matter more to the salesperson than the paycheck you potentially represent? Would you ever forget that salesperson? Would you ever buy from anyone else?

This is where Close for Life starts—establishing the standards that you want to have as a real estate professional and keeping that mindset throughout every single customer interaction. If you show your customers that they are more than a paycheck to you, they will want to come back.

CHAPTER 3

WHY YOU NEED TO KNOW YOUR STUFF

"Engage brain before opening mouth," my father used to say to me all the time. Or occasionally he went with the nicer version: "Think before you speak."

For me, the road to learning how knowing your stuff pays off started early. My dad always wanted me to learn whatever I could from older people. But because I started working when I was young, I needed to figure out how to behave in a way that would earn people's respect and be taken seriously.

My dad encouraged me to follow around the tradespeople that came to fix the equipment in the cafeteria where I worked. He told me to pay attention and try to help but most importantly to try to learn and see what they would teach me. If a plumber, electrician, air-conditioning guy, or any other craftspeople were around, there I was following them, trying not to be seen as a pesky little kid, but instead someone they would be willing to let help and share their knowledge with.

I learned that if I asked smart questions that showed I was paying attention, they were much more willing to share their information with me. My father told me many times that "once I knew something, it was mine forever. No one could steal it from me." If that's true, why wouldn't I try to learn as much as I could?

The payoff for all this study of the trades came later on. As I got older, and knew more about how things worked and what the tradespeople did, I understood the time and expense involved in repairs and other work. So, when workers came by that didn't know me and gave us an inflated estimate or suggested a nonsense repair, I could stop them in their tracks. Usually, I would cut this off at the pass by letting them know what diagnostic work I had done and what I thought the issue was. This let them know right away that they weren't going to get the fastball by me so they should not even try.

Here's an example that always makes me smile. Over the course of a year after I graduated high school, I decided to go to auto tech school and take the ASE (automotive service excellence) certification program just to learn something in my spare time. I never thought about being a mechanic but always thought it would be nice to know.

Years later when I owned my restaurants, a young woman that worked for me as a server called me up from one of the big chain repair shops where she had taken her car for service. The employees there told her that her car needed all sorts of brake work and that the bill would be over $1,800. I drove over to try to see if I could help.

When I got there, I asked for a list of what needed to be done. One of the things on the list was replacing the brake rotors. I walked into the shop and asked the tech to pull up the specs for the manufacturer on the minimum thickness for the brake rotors. He did, and I looked at the tolerances and I asked what the rotors measured, and he got really sheepish. I asked him where his micrometer (the tool used to measure how thick they are) was. He said he let someone borrow it. I told him to get it back and let's measure them together. He said that the rotors were within tolerance to be resurfaced; he was just trying to be extra cautious. The bill for the brakes went from $1,800 to $495. When you know your stuff, they can't mess with you.

This curiosity that my father instilled served me well in the beginning of my real estate career, as the market in 2008 was unlike any before. Even the most veteran agents were struggling to figure out how to make things work. Short sales were making up the lion's share of the market, but few people knew how to do them, the banks included, and so we had to learn on the fly how to get things done. I committed myself to learning all I could about short sales. It worked. I went from being brand-new agent to having more than 70 active listings at a time within my first two years in the business. That all came from being curious and taking nothing for granted.

I asked my attorney about short sale laws and asked the short sale processors exactly how the process worked. I learned enough to make their jobs easier. In short order, I was seen as a short sale expert to the point that other agents would just give me listings because they didn't want to handle them.

THE CUSTOMER MINDSET

If you're an agent, you're familiar with this scenario: The customers come into your office thinking they probably know more about the market than the majority of agents, including you. After all, they have seen stuff on the internet, watched HGTV, and even read a half a blog post about real estate once. Remember from the previous chapter, most customers don't think much of agents. The customers figure if they do a little research, it'll make them smarter and more informed than you.

As agents, to counteract all this, we must know our product thoroughly and know how to use that knowledge to stop know-it-all customers in their tracks.

For instance, you should know that residential real estate mortgage interest rates are not based on the rate the Federal Reserve sets (the federal funds rate is the rate that banks lend money to banks—it's not the mortgage rate) but are instead based on the yield of the 10-year Treasury note. So, as an agent, you need to stay on top of what is happening to the 10-year Treasury note.

When having an initial discussion with potential customers, it's easy to drop into the conversation what the most recent trends have been on the yield of the 10-year Treasury and how it has a direct impact on the interest rate the customers will pay on their mortgage. This same information could be used with sellers in a listing presentation when discussing the current market environment for buyers and where mortgage rates are going.

This is just one little piece of information that gives me a tremendous ability to create a very different sounding conversation from that of the average agent. In my experience, more than 95 percent of agents don't understand how mortgage rates are determined. Yet consistently nearly 80 percent of all home purchases are bought with financing. That means four out of five of my customers are affected by this information, but most agents can't be bothered to figure out how interest rates work. They are too busy monitoring their Instagram feed or posting pictures of themselves at a closing.

News flash! They aren't hiring you for a freaking photo op at the closing. They are hiring you because you are supposed to know what the heck you're doing. No, there is nothing wrong with taking photos at the closing, but you need to have your house in order too. Most agents need to post the closing pictures to attract new customers to replace the ones at the closing who will be using a different agent next time. Do you think that's harsh? Less than 12 percent of customers use the same agents a second time. That is abysmal and truly inexcusable.

The recipe for success is really very simple and consists of only two jobs:

Job 1. Know what the heck you are doing.

Job 2. Market yourself as someone who knows what the heck you are doing.

Our industry does this in reverse. Most agents wind up being so busy doing Job 2 (which they have made Job 1) that they never actually get around to Job 1. As an individual, you need to commit to being the goods. The customers want a market expert—someone who gets how this thing works. They come to us because they don't know how to do this. If that is the case, what exactly is the market demand that we need to meet? *Answer:* We need to actually know how the market works.

We will talk more about getting the customer right later, but for now your mindset needs to be how to get yourself right and how to know what you are talking about.

Current events are always a wellspring of opportunities to show that you know what you are talking about. For example, as I am writing this chapter, inflation is on the rise. That's a Pandora's box for the economy and interest rates, and something we can talk about to customers. We can talk about what causes inflation and how the Fed is fighting it (with interest rate hikes). We can discuss the possibility of a recession and how that will affect the price of real estate, both residential and commercial.

Yes, as a residential agent you should have an opinion about commercial real estate and not act like it is somehow anathema to discuss it. You are supposed to be a real estate professional. You need to know your market. Customers need you to be a trusted advisor, not a transaction facilitator. One of those two roles tends to have repeat business, and the other is immensely replaceable. Care to guess which is which?

If you're not filling the trusted advisor role, do not be surprised to find out that your customers are cheating on you with other agents behind your back. You've given them full license to cheat because there is nothing you have provided them that they can't get some-place else. If you are seen as replaceable by the customers, don't be surprised when they do just that.

BE PASSIONATE

To know your stuff, you need to be curious about your product and the market. This means treating real estate like something you are interested in. It blows my mind when agents start talking about their hobbies and they can rattle off statistics, model numbers, distances, countries of manufacturing, and a million other obscure factoids that interest them, but yet they can't be bothered to be interested in the very thing that they are depending upon to be their source of income to pay for those hobbies. Getting your head on right with this means making real estate into something you are passionate about.

There are lots of ways to supplement what you know. Read books on the history of real estate. Read news stories and see if you can fig-ure out how current events will affect real estate. Another really great tool is audiobooks. The nature of our business has lots of car time. Using that time to listen to books that supplement your knowledge base, rather than just jamming out to the latest tunes, is an invest-ment in your future and your future customers' experience of working with you. There are many audiobooks covering topics like economics, investment, and history that can give you great context for what you see going on today.

Basic Economics by Thomas Sowell was invaluable to me in clar-ifying how the law of supply and demand works, what makes a market, and what pressures affect the economy. I started closing a lot more deals when I stopped wasting my downtime listening to political rants and music and instead focused on things that would help customers. Start taking advantage of time the other agents are wasting. It will give you a market advantage that will only grow with time.

Here's another really crazy idea to help. Buy some of the stuff you are trying to sell people. Agents who own real estate tend to be very aware of the things that affect their properties. This is especially true of agents who buy investment property. If you want to be much more interested in real estate, the solution may be as simple as going through the process of investing in it yourself.

Stop just making your customers rich. If you follow the age-old saying "put your money where your mouth is," real estate probably will become much more interesting to you. Suddenly, you'll no longer be an outside observer of the market; you'll be an active participant. Of course, not everyone in real estate can afford to invest in properties, but getting there should be a major goal in your business. Being involved as a principal gives you a visceral sense of the market that non-investors typically just can't compete with.

LEARN TO NEGOTIATE

While market knowledge is essential, it isn't the only thing you need to understand to be good at real estate. I know what you are thinking. "Great, Josh, keep piling on more stuff we need to know." Folks, this is the stuff I actually needed to know, as opposed to all the other garbage some people told me I needed to be successful in this business.

A big place where you need to constantly be learning and improving is negotiation. One of the things that drove me up a wall with real estate negotiation classes is they all are overwhelmingly focused on collaborative negotiation. Collaborative negotiations are great, as long as there is a collaborative negotiator on the other side. If not, you are going to lose your shirt, socks, and more.

If you don't know how to negotiate both collaboratively and competitively, you are not prepared to defend your customers' interest regardless of what type of negotiator you face. In other words, you can help in some negotiations but not all. The issue is agents don't typically recuse themselves when they realize they are out of their depth. They follow the mainstream real estate philosophy of keep faking it till you make it baby!

If you're overmatched in a negotiation, you will fail your customers. They won't get what they need from the deal. The experience of working with you will leave them feeling underwhelmed, to say the least, and they will probably not want to work with you in the future. That's not how to close your customers for life.

Agents get very touchy about this and will complain about competitive negotiators. That seems to extend from the adage that if you can't beat them, complain about them behind their back ('cause that'll show them who's boss). I am not telling you to always negotiate competitively. Collaborative negotiations are definitely preferable, as both sides tend to walk away happier. But if the situation calls for it, you need to have the capacity to "bring the thunder."

My policy is that if the agent is nice and is willing to negotiate collaboratively, then I will be all in with that approach. If the agent starts to negotiate competitively, well, you mess with the bull, you get the horns. Most of the time I find that when I push back hard and show that if anyone gets run over, it won't be me, the other agent all of a sudden wants to negotiate collaboratively. Funny how building a little bit of respect alters the way people treat us, isn't it? Maybe we can use that tool later to figure out how to get our customers to value us more. First, let me give you an example of how this can be used to actually close deals and customers for life.

THE ROCK T-SHIRT GUY

About five years ago, I met a mother and son team who owned and operated a business that they were looking to sell. They had two after-school care facilities, as well as owning the real estate the buildings were on. So, this was a "business brokerage with real estate" deal. They had a great rapport with the agent they were working with; they had even invited her over for dinner. But she couldn't close the deal. The clients wanted to sell, but they refused to provide financials on what the businesses were actually bringing in, and the negotiation seemed to have reached an impasse. The agent could sense that they were about to jump ship, and she decided to ask me for help to resuscitate the relationship and get something she could sell.

To me this was, on its face, a fairly easy negotiation. If they do not provide the financials, then any buyer is going to consider this a riskier purchase. The higher the risk, the lower the purchase price will be. If you want top dollar for the property, then we are going to need to remove as much risk from the buyer's side as we can. That was the case I thought I was going to need to make.

Notice how I said "thought." When I negotiate, I'm on high alert and paying attention. I need as much data as I can get on the people I'm talking to and what they're looking for.

As I walked into the room, I immediately took stock of the scene. The agent who had asked for my help was sitting at the head of the table, with the mother on one side and her son across from her. The mother was an elegant woman in her seventies, and the son was in his mid-to-late thirties, in a rock T-shirt, slouching in his chair, with a wise guy haircut and a thick silver chain around his neck. He was an easy read: I could tell that he had a high opinion of himself. As I entered, he was the one doing all the talking. This was a clear indicator to me that he was the primary decision maker and therefore the person I needed to deal with.

As the agent introduced me, the son turned and said, "Josh, if you can't give us an open listing, get the hell out." That was hello. The next part of our conversation went something like this:

Me: "Open listing. Cool. How do you feel about open marriages?"

Him: "I feel pretty good about them."

Me: "Let me ask you a question. How much loyalty do you really expect from your partner in an open marriage?"

Him, smiling: "Sit down."

I earned my seat at the table that day by knowing how to play the player. We wound up talking about a bunch of other stuff, and it turned out that the mother owned 10 condos all over Miami Beach. She was rolling in dough, and she owned them all for cash.

I said to them, "My God, why don't you borrow some money? Get long in real estate right now, guys."

I got the financial calculator out on my phone and showed them the kind of returns they could be making. So, now this guy is getting ready to sign the contract. He's got the pen in his hand and is ready to go. Then just as ink starts to meet paper, he puts the pen down and gives me this half little jackass smile. And he says, "So, why should we use you?"

I slid my cell phone with the calculator still open, with his projected returns on it, across the table, and I said, "Because I'm the only guy you know that can come in here and do the numbers right in front of your face without being scared to make a mistake. You don't know anybody else like that. Sign the papers, and let's cut the crap." Listing agreement signed. Done.

Now, I'd normally never do that with a customer, but this was a bespoke solution to an individual problem. That customer, as much of a jackass as he was, needed that from me. That customer would only respond to strength. He was never going to respect an agent that didn't have the ability to push back hard and stand up to him. If I didn't show him that, he would assume that everybody else would walk all over me. And you want to know something? He would have been right. I was auditioning for him right then and there on how I would represent him in the future.

If you don't know your stuff, you are doomed to a terrible fate. You become replaceable, forgettable, or interchangeable. I don't know about you, but I don't aspire to be any of those things. If instead you have a conversation with a customer and the customer, at any point, says, "Huh, I didn't know that," you have accomplished something important. You have proved that you are the keeper of wisdom, that you know your stuff well enough to provide something of value. That's not easily replaceable, forgettable, or interchangeable.

If you can do that, then customers will take their hard-earned money and happily hire you. That's how you close your customers for life.

CHAPTER 4

HOW TO FIND YOUR NICHE

One of the most important things in life to figure out is what we are here on earth to do. All of us seem to have certain skills or gifts that make us suited to do something with excellence. Some folks identify their "calling" when they are young, but for many of us, much of our adult life is spent trying to figure out what we are going to do when we grow up. My brother had a calling to study philosophy and ethics and eventually become a college professor. For me, I had no clue what I was supposed to do for much of my adult life. I had worked with a bunch of tradespeople for years and had finally developed some proficiency and liked finding something I was good at.

When I was about 15 years old, I told my father that I had decided I really enjoyed working outside with my hands, and that is what I wanted to do with myself. I liked using power tools and building stuff on our 2½-acre property. It didn't bother me to be dirty, and I liked the feeling of accomplishment after completing a physical task.

After telling my father of this interest, guess what he did the next day? He reassigned me to work in the office. As you might imagine, I was thoroughly pissed off. I had just told him I liked being outside and working with my hands, and he sticks me in the freaking office! It's like, "Why the hell did I even bother telling you? Should I have lied?"

To make matters worse, he had me take over the inventory controls for our entire operation and reconcile bank statements (to add insult to injury). For those of you keeping score at home, this is about as far away from the carpentry I enjoyed as one could get.

The thing was, my dad knew me, and he saw my potential. While I complained about the move, I still did the work. It turned out I was really good with the inventory. I was able to cut the amount of inventory we needed to carry by over 40 percent and reduce the times we went out of stock. I was also good at reconciling the company bank statements. If my dad had not forced me to try new things, I may have gone through my life never knowing what I was capable of and falling short of what I have been able to learn, enjoy, and achieve.

But what my dad was really doing was teaching me to be a man for all seasons. When the chips are down, are you going to say, "Oh, sorry—that's actually not my department . . ." No. Regardless of whether you like it or not, things need to be done, and someone needs to step up and do them. He wanted me to be the type of guy who could step up no matter what the problem was and say, "Put me in, coach! I can handle this."

My dad practiced what he preached. If things went wrong in the plant, he would tear the sleeves off his shirt and go to work with the guys to get it done. He didn't allow himself to sit back and avoid grunt work just because he was the boss. My dad learned this from my grandfather.

BROADEN YOUR HORIZONS

This building of capacity shows you what you have to work with within yourself. Exposing yourself to things that you may not think you will like is an important step to finding your niche in any business.

I always advise people just starting in any industry to take a handful of diverse classes in the field and take stock of what different areas feel like. Which were the easiest to get through? Which were the ones that made you look at your watch the fewest number of times? To carve out your niche, you need to find the intersection between what interests you, what you're naturally good at, and what the industry needs. At first, that niche might be quite narrow. But as you develop and gain hands-on experience in the industry, you can focus on handling more things and broadening your niche.

When you attend classes, make sure to participate. Many times, I will give an investment class, and a couple of sourpuss agents will sit there and refuse to download the financial calculator until more than halfway through the class because they came in with their mind made up to be bored. They feel this way because they think this experience will be like so many others they have had where there is nothing there to learn. This sort of cynicism is rampant in the industry. Unfortunately for the sourpusses, they missed out on some of the most important information. So go in with an attitude to learn anything you can. Remember, you are taking time away from money-making activities to be there, so do whatever you can to give yourself a return on that investment.

Also, take the chance to work with any quality agents you can. Many times, things you don't understand or can't stand doing are only that way for you because of the person that taught you. Finding people to work with who are good at what they do, are passionate about it, and are good teachers is worth its weight in gold.

One of the best ways to get people to want to work with you and share what they know is to be genuinely interested in what they do. Approach them with "wide-eyed wonder" about how they do what they do, and never worry about splitting a commission to further your education. Learn to be as helpful as possible too, and try to provide as much value as you can in exchange for a seasoned agent's help. For many rock star agents, if you simply handle the time frames and paperwork for them, that can be seen as a huge blessing and makes them enjoy working with you and simultaneously teaching you the tricks of the trade.

Another thing you want to make sure of is to not prioritize your commission split over a good work environment and great training. Finding a brokerage that teaches well is very important for new agents. And let's be honest—there are plenty of not-so-new agents that could use some training as well.

Make sure your brokerage work environment is conducive to finding and establishing your niche. You need a place where you are comfortable and productive and that helps you maintain your standards. If your brokerage is a source of frustration, then you need to assess if that is because you are a problem or it is. If it's you, cut it out and play nice. If it's the brokerage, leave and find a place that plays nice. Your brokerage should be something that frees up your bandwidth to build your business and find your niche.

HOW I FOUND MY NICHE

When I entered real estate, I didn't know what area to focus on. I was lucky to wind up at a great brokerage with Drew Epstein, a broker that became a good friend. Working there allowed me to see the opportunities with short sales, and I was encouraged to jump all over those sales as a way to get my business going in a hurry. It served its purpose, and I really enjoyed helping people get out of being upside down and losing their homes.

Unfortunately, the short sale niche only existed because of the housing collapse of 2008 and therefore had a limited shelf life. I needed to find something for which the market would have a long-term demand. Partnering also served me well in my early career. When a seasoned agent worked a deal with me, I did my best to handle as much as I could. I wanted the agent I was working with to not even think or hear about it again until the broker called to give the agent the check. Both partnering and learning the short sale business got me established, but neither was the long-term solution to my need to find my niche.

I tried many different things seeking to find the things that came naturally and easily for me. If I enjoyed them, that wouldn't be so bad either. Over time, I started carving out a niche in bringing commercial real estate analysis to the residential side of the business.

In my effort to find my niche, I learned a lot of tools used for large projects that had big price tags and major investors. Things like differential cash flows, capital accumulation, and capital stacks—which were never available to the small investor. Exposing myself to this meant that I could give the under-5-unit investors the same experience as the guys that are buying 5,000 units. That knowledge made me stand out, to the point where other agents sent those types of clients to me. Or they brought me in on deals that I otherwise would have had nothing to do with because they knew I would make the investor feel more comfortable. Either way, the business came to me, with no outside effort on my part.

People see what I do now and think it must be so nice to know all this stuff. They forget that I wasn't born with this knowledge (obviously). When I started in the business, I knew that I didn't know nearly enough, and it scared the hell out of me. Why should the customer trust me with a transaction if I didn't even trust myself? I spent those first two years in real estate trying to be as much of an information sponge as possible. I took every course I could get my hands on, trying to understand the entire ecosystem of the business—not just the basic MLS stuff. I wanted to know how various pieces worked together and where the opportunities were.

In all those classes I took, there were several dogs in there. Classes that were just boring as sin and not very helpful. Some were good, but many were at best marginal. Yet I do not regret taking any of them. The exposure to these classes allowed me to see many things that are missing from mainstream real estate education. That has allowed me to find the niche I enjoy today of helping agents to find the missing pieces to their puzzles.

Outside of real estate, there are many things I thought I would hate, but once I tried them, I was pleasantly surprised that I liked them: escargot, ballroom dancing, and board games. Too bad I was stubborn and missed out for years on things that I really enjoy.

KEYS TO FINDING YOUR NICHE

To summarize, here are the steps to finding your niche:

- Expose yourself to as many different facets of the business as possible.
- Take a wide variety of classes (even on things you might not think you'll like).
- Have a good attitude.
- Be curious and always learning.
- Partner with experienced agents.
- Find a brokerage that doesn't steal your bandwidth.
- Pay attention to things you like and you pick up easily.
- Be on the lookout for things the market needs and would reward.
- Carve out your niche based upon the standards you have set for your business and life.

In closing, when in pursuit of finding your niche, don't be a jackass like me. In my business, I resisted like a stubborn mule writing things. I hated writing papers in school. I embraced that self-limiting belief that "I hate writing."

If you don't get the irony in reading that line in a book I am writing, just wait a minute—it's there, I promise. This is actually the second book—that is not a textbook—I have written. In addition, I have written over 35 textbooks. I can tell you that writing is not my favorite thing, but it is definitely part of this niche that I have discovered and love.

Another donkey topic for me was public speaking. "Nope, not gonna do it. I hate it." Well, guess what? I speak all over the country (more days now than not), and I love it too. Coaching was another one I resisted tooth and nail. "Not coach material," I told myself. This is the newest and frankly one of the most rewarding of the things I do in my work. Getting the chance to help people with the individual challenges they face in this tough business and then seeing their improvement is amazing.

My resistance to trying things I thought I'd dislike delayed me from finding the things I am most passionate about doing today. The fact that some of the things I was most convinced that I hated make up the lion's share of what I love to do every day is not lost on me. It is proof positive of two things:

1. We often don't know ourselves as well as we think we do.
2. God has a very real sense of humor.

So, don't be stubborn like me. Be open to new things. Question why you hate the things you think you hate, and be willing to try those things again with an open mind. You may just find the part of this business you wind up doing and being most passionate about is one that you previously wrote off because you were certain it wasn't your cup of tea. Finding a niche is a worthwhile pursuit of seeking the best use for the way that you are made. If a hammer is happiest when hammering a nail, then finding your niche is very much about figuring out what kind of nail you hammer best.

CHAPTER 5

HOW TO GET THE BEST OUT OF YOURSELF

O ne day I was with my dad, and some folks were discussing what their kids were going to grow up to do. One guy said his son wanted to grow up to be a doctor. Another fellow said his son wanted to be a lawyer. I clearly remember my dad turning to me and saying, "Son, I don't care if you grow up to be a floor sweeper. You just be the best damn floor sweeper there is. It doesn't matter whose floor it is you are sweeping. When you sweep that floor, it is your floor. The way that you sweep that floor is an indication of who you are and the type of work you will do."

Taking ownership of our standards and headspace and understanding that we are responsible for what we produce is very important. It removes the biggest issue from the table that traps most people into mediocrity: excuses. People look at things that come up in life, and rather than ask, "Can this be overcome?," instead ask, "Do I have a good enough excuse so that people will give me a pass to justify not doing this thing?" In other words, we are looking for a reason to not get something done. This is especially true when dealing with the number one person that represents a stumbling block to our success: ourselves.

The person looking back at you in the mirror will be your biggest challenge to achieving success. You are the one who doesn't do what you tell yourself you are going to do. You are the one that makes excuses. There are a lot of good excuses out there. There are plenty of people you could blame. You know what? It might even be their fault. Who gives a rat's ass? You can't do a damn thing about them. Any time you spend wishing, hoping, and moaning that they will change is a waste of time.

You can, however, do something about you. Dispense with excuses. "The customers weren't serious, so that is why I didn't close them," "I don't have the time to make the calls because people don't answer," or "They were some kind of 'ist' [racist, sexist, etc.], and that's why they chose someone else." The reality is that's garbage you let yourself believe to dull the pain of failure. It gives you an excuse to not have to improve. You are justified to sit there and complain instead of taking action to get what you can get out of the situation.

The Yankees played the Cleveland Indians in the 1998 American League Championship Series. A ball was hit out in front of the plate, and the catcher grabbed it and tossed it to first base. As it sailed toward the base, it bounced off the runner. As the second baseman (who had been covering first base) turned to the umpire to complain, two more runs scored. The second baseman's actions mirror how a lot of people behave today. When something goes wrong, they immediately look to blame someone else rather than taking accountability themselves. Meanwhile, opportunities pass them by while they yell at life's umpires about how unfair their situation is. But does it really do them any good to think this way?

The thought process to get yourself mentally prepared to make progress is to start looking at your excuse-making self as the enemy.

I know that I will be the one most capable of sabotaging myself if I let my excuse maker start his nonsense. I need to cut it off before it starts. So, waking up, look at yourself in the mirror and say, "We meet again, old foe. Today there will be no excuses. Today is a day of accountability and victory."

This may seem like some kind of self-loathing—but it comes from a good place. It is based on respect for your ability to overcome and adapt. It also recognizes that those muscles have to be exercised. We need to push ourselves to identify and reject our excuses and embrace taking action to improve.

PARTICIPATION TROPHIES DON'T CUT IT

Our self-loving, self-embracing, self-esteem–inflating society doesn't believe in accountability, and this is to everyone's detriment. Participation trophies don't make us consider what we did wrong or what we could have done better. A participation trophy is an excuse. It changes the goal from winning to showing up. This means that there is no need to consider what you did, as you have been rewarded, so you did good enough. A participation trophy is only meaningful to a person who lost. If you won, that is what you want to be acknowledged for, and it should be. Not that you simply showed up.

Acknowledging the win gives credit to the work that went into the win and makes us consider what the winner did to succeed. If we instead give the participation trophy, it just rebrands the loss as a quasi-win. We know in our hearts it's garbage, but it makes it easier to stomach, so we keep lying to ourselves. What participation trophies do adults use? Phrases like:

- "Well, I tried my best." (Very seldom is that true, and we know it.)

- "I've tried, and I just can't." (The ultimate self-fulfilling proph-
  ecy that justifies failure. I did try, so therefore I am relieved of
  the responsibility to try anymore.)
- "The universe has conspired against me, so I can't fight the
  whole universe, right?" (Taking refuge in the idea that some
  things just aren't meant to be.)
- Then there is the "I'm not good enough" family of excuses: "I
  am genetically unable to, so I get a pass." See some siblings
  below:
  ○ "I'm not smart enough."
  ○ "I'm not good at math."
  ○ "I'm not good at _____."

I had so many of these in my life, I probably can't even count
them. But so you don't feel like you can use the participation trophy
of "He's just one of those lucky people that it's easy for," here goes a
list of some of mine:

- I am terrified of public speaking. My knees shake to the point
  I can't stand when I try to talk to a group of people.
- I am a massive introvert that doesn't like people.
- I am a failure in business.
- I can't type or write anything longer than an email.
- I'm scared of roller coasters.
- I'm lazy.
- I'll always be overweight.
- I can't dance and have no rhythm (and don't even have the
  guilty-feet excuse).

This is a short list. Pretty sure if I started asking my family members
for feedback, this would be the longest chapter in this book.

Some of this stuff is more serious than others, but all were personal struggles that I had to fight with myself to overcome. I'll tell
you the truth. I put up a hell of a fight not to change. Sometimes it

went on for years, but the feeling of winning on the most hard fought of these battles was incredibly sweet. I want you to have that feeling too.

One battle that I was terrified of for years was learning to dance. I hate looking like an idiot in front of people. I was paralyzed by the thought I would be dumbest-looking kid in dance class—so I never tried. I always knew I would like a version of me that could dance better than a version that didn't, but my fear and self-limiting beliefs kept me from taking the steps to change, even though it was something completely within my control.

Eventually in my early twenties, my mom (the only person I ever casually mentioned that it might be something I might want to do) bought me some lessons, and a love affair began. I wish I could tell you it was easy, and I was some sort of savant. Instead, let's just say the short bus took me to dance class for quite a while. None of it came easy to me, but I stuck with it and became a competition-level ballroom dancer.

It opened up opportunities to me that I would not have had otherwise, and it became one of my most effective ways to exercise and relieve stress. That was nice, but the most important thing about learning to dance was that it proved to me that if I pushed myself, I could slay my inner dragons. So, if and when a dragon came along that really mattered, I already knew I was the kind of person who could slay dragons.

You can accomplish so much more when you stop lying to yourself and start embracing personal accountability. The idea of being perfect the way you are is complete nonsense. We came into this world pooping on ourselves and not knowing how to eat food without wearing it. We had to learn to use a bathroom and silverware. That training was required to be accepted into society. What makes you think that process ended when we got older? Did learning to ride a bike happen on the first try? Some things will be harder to overcome than others. It will take effort and practice to get there. The only way to do it is to stop giving yourself participation trophies and to start putting in the work. Stop depriving yourself and the world of who you are capable of being.

BUILD A WINNING RECORD

Two of my coaching clients had issues with getting ahead professionally. One would be productive for a short burst and then default to some excuse: "Oh well, my doctor says . . . and I have this to do, and this other thing to do, so I can't right now . . ." The other had genuine trauma and things that happened to tank his confidence. It manifested in his customer interactions, where he didn't feel like he had the ability to take up space and stand up for himself. I helped both clients see that they were making excuses, whether intentionally or unintentionally, that were holding them back. As soon as they recognized and acknowledged that, they had huge breakthroughs.

You are responsible for you. You get the choice to complain about what has happened to you and use it as an excuse for how life isn't fair. You can check out and accept that some things just aren't meant to be. Or the other option is you can make up your mind to fight like hell to get whatever you can out of yourself. To push as far as you can, for as long as you can, until you know you can't go any further—and then take one step more.

I can paralyze myself with my thought life, which empowers adverse circumstances to control my future, or I can take my lumps in the present, deal with the fallout, and then learn whatever I can from it. Bad things that happened already suck; do I really want to extend their suckiness into my own future? Human beings grow the most from the bad things they survive. We don't grow from the good times. So, while bad things do suck, they are also opportunities to grow. The choice of paralysis or perseverance is a real one and is totally in your control.

Finding opportunities to test yourself and show your mettle is a great tool to build the mental toughness to persevere when times are tough. There have been many things in my life like the ballroom dancing above that were major obstacles to overcome. The real heart of a winner though is forged in the smaller daily battles. Getting out of your own way requires not letting your losses define you and establishing yourself as a winner. You do this by fighting the small battles and tallying the wins from them. This starts to change your perception from one who loses the battles with yourself to someone with a winning record.

You start to look in the mirror and see a person looking back at you that does what you tell yourself you are going to do. You start to really respect the person you are. Not because of the impressive array of participation trophies you have accumulated, but because of the long series of small wins you have accumulated that have led to the big wins. That self-respect just leads to more confidence and more winning.

The opportunities can come in many forms. Staying late to finish one more task than you usually would is you winning by getting more out of yourself. Going to the gym after a grueling day at the office when no one would blame you if you skipped is another. Setting a goal to make 30 calls in a day and making 35 because you are the kind of person that not just meets your goals—you surpass them. All of these are the places to start collecting those wins. You want to find as many ways as you can to compete with yourself and win so you can start building your winning record. The one caveat is that the wins must push you. They don't have to shatter your previous paradigms, but they should push you. If they don't, you will know it and not respect it. We need you to learn to respect all that you bring to the table.

I had learned this lesson, as I mentioned earlier, the hard way in 2008, when all my assets were wiped out. Lenders made bad loans. Banks changed their lending criteria. The government pushed everybody to buy a home. Politicians on both sides of the aisle encouraged people to invest in real estate. Could I have blamed all these people for my losses? I had ample excuses, but the reality was, I got myself into a position where I was hurt by the economic meltdown. I made the choice to take the loans that I did. Instead of living a life of bitterness about what had happened, I made the choice to say to myself, "Look—that was Wednesday. Bad things happened. But today is Thursday. So, what the hell are you going to do about it?"

Embracing that mentality was what led me to real estate and allowed me to start building the portfolio I have now. The moral of the story is that if you don't like where you are, stop blaming other people. Acknowledge that the reason you are where you are is because of you. If you want something different, you're going to have to start demanding something different from *you*. If you're waiting for other people to change, you're wasting your time.

Every day of your life you are given a beautiful gift: a blank page on which you have the opportunity to write the next installment in the history of your life. The future of your life will be shaped by what you write today. If you want a better future, and you don't like your past, start writing differently than you have in the past. When you embrace this truth, it only makes sense to choose the finest inks, the best words, and a calligrapher's pen to fill the pages. You choose what you write. Will it be a story of missed opportunities or a story of adversities overcome? Will you embrace accountability and eliminate the excuses that distract from realizing that the only one keeping your story from being a masterpiece is the one writing it, which is you?

PART II

GET YOUR PRODUCT RIGHT

CHAPTER 6

WHY HAS ALL THE PRODUCT KNOWLEDGE DISAPPEARED?

" If you don't know what you are talking about, don't say anything." My father peppered me with this statement throughout my early life. It wasn't just a good piece of advice; my dad adhered to this principle throughout his life.

It was very rare that I ever asked my dad about anything that he didn't know about. If I asked about how a car worked, he wouldn't just tell me the skinny pedal makes it go and the fat one makes it stop. He would explain how the whole thing worked.

My father was never a mechanic, but he was always a guy that loved to learn. People that spoke without knowing what they were talking about were immediately branded as "not knowing their ass from a hole in the ground." That was a high crime in the world in which I grew up, and so I focused a high degree of effort on the differentiation of ground holes and my personal exit orifice. If you wanted to be respected, you knew what the heck you were talking about.

THE DECLINE
OF BROKER EDUCATION

In my classes, I often ask participants what percentage of agents they consider "bad." The answer is consistently between 80 and 95 percent. By the way, the people answering the question are agents themselves. Yikes, right? So how did we get here?

When we really trace it back, a key issue is that inflation has been working against people's wealth for decades. In other words, while we're making slightly more money, the money is worth a bit less. This means that our standard of living has actually been slightly falling for quite a while now. Especially in sales, this has made people desperate to increase their share of the pie. Agents push for higher and higher splits, taking more profit from the brokerage or whoever is in charge.

But the value of a brokerage isn't just having a comfy chair in a cushy office or a place to hang your license. There is (or at least used to be) a huge education component that brokers arranged for and provided as well. Agent development was a big part of the broker's job and the foundation of the culture of brokerage in years past.

Back then, when a new real estate agent (or lawyer, insurance broker, car salesperson, you name it) entered the industry, there was a disconnect between what they learned to become licensed and what they actually needed to know to be successful in practice. The broker or office leadership used to help fill in those knowledge gaps, particularly in helping new agents to understand customers and how to provide a good product.

For example, when I got my first listing back in 2008, I asked the person in my office with the most experience to come with me on calls so I could learn. I was happy to split the commission because I'm not a "fake it 'til you make it" type of person. That mindset is not very common among agents anymore. Getting paid and keeping as much of the commission for themselves as possible has become an all-consuming pursuit for the majority of agents. This push to maximize their commission has reduced the amount of time and money available for the kind of practical training that brokers used to provide.

The brokers are not free from blame either. The cutthroat competition between brokerages that advertise very high commission splits will frequently force otherwise well-meaning brokers to compromise their standards in order to compete and keep their agents. This has all brokerages at each other's throats and fighting for agents that play one brokerage off against the other.

In real estate, I've seen that either most brokers don't pay for any education whatsoever, or they'll occasionally bring in a speaker for a 30-minute lunch-and-learn. What the heck are you going to learn in 30 minutes? This is a business that has a bazillion facets to it. There's so much to know that it's impossible for anyone to understand everything. And the idea of mentorship programs, of sending people away for three days to take a class? That's all gone away. The onus for agents' education falls upon the agents themselves, but unfortunately most think that they don't have to continue to learn once they've passed the licensing exam.

Because of the way things have changed, the only sustainable business model is for brokers to go wide and shallow rather than narrow and deep. Those that try to focus on building and investing in great agents can't do it fast enough to generate enough commissions prior to those agents jumping ship to a brokerage offering higher commission splits. To combat that, brokers need to get bodies in chairs that can sell as fast as possible. The problem is that agents then mirror the behavior of their brokerage, treating customers as one-off relationships that don't deserve any time and energy. The result? Their customers won't come back, and the agents end up underpaid and burned out. This is a big part of the reason why nearly 90 percent of new agents leave the industry within five years.

We can also add to that mix that many of the professional organizations recognize this turnover and cater to newer agents. The constant inflow of new agents is what keeps the membership fees getting paid. Classes in lead acquisition, MLS, social media, and branding are the most popular topics in real estate education today.

THE IMPORTANCE OF UNDERSTANDING FINANCE

Where is the class on the actual product we sell, you may ask? Great question. I wondered that for years until I got frustrated enough to write one. Classes that focus on the actual nature and attributes of what real estate owners can expect from their property are just not part of real estate culture. It almost seems like everyone is looking at everyone else like, "Aren't you guys supposed to be teaching that?" Meanwhile the poor doe-eyed new agents have no idea what the hell they're doing, and there is no one to direct them where to go because the information is almost impossible to find.

The other reason for the lack of product knowledge is the disdain that mainstream education has for all things money, investment, and finance. One of the essential things to recognize about real estate transactions is that they are financial transactions, just as much as they are real estate deals. Understand that real estate usually is purchased with borrowed money, and it is often the largest investment people ever make.

Most agents don't recognize they need to have just as much knowledge of the financial and money side as they do the real estate side. The problem is financial, and investment information is not readily available in the traditional education system in the United States from kindergarten to graduate-level programs and beyond. Unless you study finance, you will be exposed to almost zero information on how money, lending, or investing actually works.

It's strange, isn't it? In a country that people around the world come to because of all the financial opportunities available, many of our own citizens have no idea how the financial system and markets actually work.

I believe the collective lack of financial knowledge begins with teachers and professors, most of whom get very little exposure to the financial system in their own educations or jobs. Sure, most teachers work very hard. Teaching is a tough job, often with demanding hours, and many take work home regularly—but the nature of the work doesn't build expertise in financial matters. This leaves teachers in a position where they can't help students to understand finance either. So, unless their parents teach them, or they learn it for themselves, teachers and students lack the knowledge base they need to understand real estate transactions and markets.

We often see this when teachers burn out in the classroom and decide to become real estate agents (which is actually very common). Typically, these agents need more financial training than other types of agents, as their teaching job didn't prepare them for understanding and explaining how the financial part of acquiring and owning the product works.

I learned this firsthand when I went to college. When I graduated from high school, I wanted nothing to do with any other schooling. I had made up my mind that I had written my last paper. Besides, I already had businesses going. I didn't need more schooling.

After starting to build back all that I lost in 2008, I decided to see what all the fuss with college was about. I took a class or two in the evenings with the honest intent to just learn as much as I could. I was paying for it out of pocket and was not eligible for any grants or aid, so I was incentivized to get my money's worth in that way too. It was a much better mindset than I previously had for school, and it made for a much more enjoyable experience.

I was genuinely surprised though by how poorly the professors understood how the world actually works. Plus, in several of my classes, the material they were supposed to teach almost took a back seat to the political proselytizing my professors felt it was their duty to do. I was bombarded with "what to think" rather than encouraged to learn "how to think." Their views were only possible because they didn't understand how markets, the economy, and financial systems work.

I can't really be mad at the professors. (Well, maybe a little annoyed. Remember the beginning of this chapter where I talked about the importance of knowing what the hell you are talking about.) When I would stay and speak with my professors after class, I saw that they didn't even know what to do with their own money, so how could they be expected to give their students good advice. It was the ultimate blind-leading-the-blind situation.

In conclusion, if you want to find out how to make money, how to understand investments, how real estate (or any other investment type) functions in various markets, or even just how supply and demand affect a market, you will need to find that information from outside sources. That puts the responsibility on you.

Understand that in-depth knowledge of finance and markets is required to truly understand what you are selling, what the customers may need to buy it, how they will be able to pay for it, what kind of risks they can expect from owning it, and what kind of return they can get on their capital.

Picking up this book shows that you have embraced the idea that the status quo is no longer acceptable to you and you're taking action. So, kudos for that.

But don't stop with this book. To succeed in real estate, you have to become a market expert. You have to acquire the knowledge that allows you to be relevant and informed so that you can genuinely help your customers and turn them into customers for life. If you don't make it a priority, no one in this industry is going to make it one for you.

CHAPTER 7

THE PROS OF REAL ESTATE

One day my dad asked me to excavate a 40- x 100-foot section of land and pour a concrete driveway. I was 15 at this point. I couldn't even drive. I asked him what to do, and he said, "Figure it out." Classic.

So, I started digging with a shovel, and I quickly discovered that it takes a lot more effort to move dirt than one might think. I called around town and found a company that inexplicably agreed to rent a backhoe to a 15-year-old (hey, I was very convincing on the phone).

To add a cherry on top of this dumpster fire of a situation, Dad said he wanted me to use a cement mixer of his that must have been from the 1930s. The thing kept breaking down while it was loaded with cement, which is problematic because the concrete will harden in the machine, and you would then need to spend some up-close and personal time with a chisel to get it out. Not fun. Also, you really want as close to a continuous pour as you can get, or the concrete will not be as strong.

Fixing the recurring issue with the cement mixer meant sticking my hand in up to my armpit to reach behind the motor and fix the part that kept breaking. I wound up with burns all over my skin. Keep in mind that prior to this project, the only concrete mixing I had done was in a bucket—like to fill in fence post holes. I was certainly no expert, but my dad said to figure it out.

About 400 bags of concrete, a few strips of skin, and maybe a few choice utterances about my father later, I went to him and said we were just finishing up the project. It was one of the few times my dad ever said that he was impressed with or proud of me. The reason why is that my father's standard was always to do great work. That's the minimum expectation; you don't get a gold star for that. But if you pulled off something he hadn't been quite sure you could execute, he would tell you so.

Truth be told, I think my dad was positioning me to learn these lessons and have all these experiences because he had a sense of his own mortality. He had lived a pretty rough life before I came around, and as the oldest, I would one day be responsible for taking care of my mom, brother, and sister. By the time he passed away in 2002, his lessons had become the foundation for success in my own right. But it wasn't until I lost everything in the market crash six years later that I was really forced to see whether the stuff Dad taught me worked or whether it was just the ravings of an old guy who had succeeded during a different time.

I share this story here because the big lesson I learned with that job was "to go figure it out." My dad to that point had always given me detailed instructions on how to do whatever he wanted me to get done. My father did this to me because he knew that the life skill of figuring stuff out is an important one, as not everyone is going to hand you what you need to know or do to succeed. That was certainly my experience in real estate, but this lesson my dad taught me with a cement mixer helped guide me to go find the answers.

We are in an industry that largely expects you to figure this stuff out for yourself. Let me save you some of the searching and bring together for you some of the more important things I had to go figure out on my own that have helped me build my business and close customers for life.

KNOW YOUR PRODUCT

To start with, if you're going to sell something, find out what's good about it and let your customers know. Apple has one of the biggest cult followings in the world, and what does that company do? It trots out the CEO on stage every year to talk about the must-have features of the new iPhone. Customers wind up camping out in tents in front of the stores just to get their hands on it a few days before everyone else.

On the other hand, when was the last time you saw any sort of real estate advertisement that talked about what's good about the product (as opposed to bragging about the brokerage, touting agents' sales numbers, or publicizing how much other listings in the neighborhood sold for)? Instead, there is an expectation that the customers must know the benefits of real estate and can decide on their own if they want to own properties. This presents a huge opportunity for agents. If you can show customers what is good about real estate, you give them a new incentive to do the deal.

An example from another industry was when I took my Chevy Yukon XL in for service in 2006. Now, I'm a pretty big car buff. As I mentioned earlier, I actually became an auto tech one year in my spare time. I knew that the new convertible Corvette had just come out. Was my service visit timing a coincidence? Eh, I'll never tell. So, while they were working on my Yukon, I went to the showroom and saw this brand-new Corvette convertible sitting right there. My inner gearhead's heart was all aflutter.

You know what comes next. You can feel the proximity sensors in your mind go off as if you are an unsuspecting wildebeest in the field minding your own business and the hunter, I mean salesperson, starts pursuing the prey. You know that impending sense of dread you get when you see the salesperson coming, smiling from ear to ear with hand outstretched, and you know your moment of pure enjoyment and vehicular admiration has come to a close at the car dealership that day? It was like this guy knew I was trying not to drool over the car. "Pretty nice one, isn't it?" he said as he sidled over.

"It is," I responded. "But let me stop you there, all right? I know that most of these places have a rotation system. Usually when someone walks in, the salesperson next in the queue gets that person. So go make up something terrible about me so you don't lose your spot."

"Here's the thing. I'm a New Yorker," I continued. "You're not going to sell me something. All right? Nobody sells a New Yorker. It's almost an official unwritten rule. If you get sold something, you're a schmuck."

You know what the salesperson did next? He said, "Well, I won't be up again for a while in the rotation no matter what I tell them, so I can at least let you check this one out."

He proceeded to explain this car to me in such detail and with such joy, you could tell he loved it. Even though I said point blank that I wasn't a prospective customer, he started telling me about the one he had just bought himself and showed it to me along with his stuff in the trunk. He told me about how quickly the power top went down while the car was in gear and driving, the separate engine in the front, the transmission in the rear, the near 50/50 weight distribution, the keyless entry that didn't require the keys to come out of your pocket, and the push-button keyless starter (this was 2006, so all this stuff was like magic back then). He also showed me the heads-up display in the windshield (like a fighter jet) and how it would display the number of lateral Gs you were pulling in a turn. For a car guy, this stuff was catnip.

I bought a car that day, but I did so not because I was "sold." I bought a car that day because this guy knew his stuff. He knew the car. He knew what he was selling. He knew what was good about it. He was talking to a car guy who knew cars, and he knew his stuff well enough to modify his conversation to meet me where I was. OK, fine. Did I get sold? Technically, yes. But I got sold by somebody that wasn't using sales techniques on me. He was just telling me about a car that he thought was awesome.

I understand that his ideal outcome was for me to buy a car, but his pitch came from a place of general product knowledge and love. He didn't earn that sale through scamming me into a purchase. If I had gotten that sense, I would have been out the door. It was a joy for him to sell it, and I could pick up on his genuine enthusiasm. That product knowledge is critical, unless you're selling something that genuinely sucks. And if you are selling something that genuinely sucks, start selling something else.

That begets an obvious question: Is real estate a good product, or should you start selling something else? The massive turnover in the industry would lead you to think that real estate is not a very good product, and when agents realize that, they move on to a different profession. In fact, it is quite the opposite. Real estate is so good that we get away without ever talking about what is good about it, and we still have people buying it faster than builders are making more of it.

The fact is, most of our customers don't know everything good about real estate, and agents don't know much more than the customers. This puts us in a blind-leading-the-blind situation, which is frustrating for all parties. Agents get frustrated that they can't get customers to commit to deals, which leads them to quit and try their hand at something else.

Most real estate agents view their customers' motivation levels as static. So, when agents perceive that an individual customer isn't very motivated, they think they need to go get a new, more motivated customer. Why not start with the customers you have and see if their motivation level can't be improved?

Here is a simple example: I can show a customer why buying a $325,000 piece of property to live in can save the person over $60,000 within five years compared with renting the same property at $2,550 per month. For those still keeping score at home, that is over $12,000 per year, which is more than $1,000 per month. Would anyone reading this take a $1,000-a-month raise for doing nothing?

By the way, that calculation includes me adding a $200-per-month reserve ($2,400 per year) onto the monthly payment so that the owner has a budget to repair and replace things in the home. This is as fair an assessment as I can do. If I can show people the numbers for that, I have a competitive edge. Most agents can't do this.

The idea of offering the customer a comparison is an important and often ignored aspect of the business. If I want customers to buy real estate, I need to know that I am asking them to take a shorter position (have less of) in cash in order to take a longer position in real estate. If I am telling them to sell and not buy another piece of real estate, I am advising them to make the opposite bet.

All of this seems obvious and simple, but it brings up two areas of understanding that we in real estate need to have in order to make that comparison. We need to be able to answer this question: What is the outlook for the real estate properties under consideration, and how does that compare with the outlook for being in cash? The place to start would be to have a better understanding of the basic properties of real estate, which are separated here into positive and negative points.

THE PROS AND CONS
OF REAL ESTATE

Agents must be able to explain the advantages and disadvantages of buying and owning real estate to their customers.

Here are a few of the advantages:

The Pros

- Lack of volatility
- Consistent appreciation
- A natural hedge against inflation
- Tax advantages:
  - Tax-free profits of up to $250,000 for an individual and $500,000 for a married couple (primary residence only)
  - Tax deduction for mortgage interest
  - Depreciation (for investment properties)
  - Capital gains (for investment properties)
  - 1031 exchange (for investment properties)
- Cash flow (for investment properties)
- Inexpensive to finance (relative to other investments)
- Long-term fixed-rate financing available
- Tangible
- Utility
- One of the greatest wealth-building tools ever invented

And now for the disadvantages:

The Cons

- Lack of liquidity
- Tangible (it has problems too)
- Tenants (for investment properties)
- Repairs

- Leasing (for investment properties)
- Possibility of higher interest rates hurting buying power

Let's start unpacking these one at a time and see if we can see how each of these affects our product. We'll talk about the pros of real estate first. The next chapter will discuss the cons.

THE PROS EXPLAINED

These are the great things about your product that your customers should know. You want to work these into the conversation when discussing what they would like to do in the market.

Lack of Volatility

Real estate has provided as consistent and dependable value and growth as any other product in existence. The stock market makes multiple percentage point swings from day to day. Real estate swings are measured in months and years.

When Covid hit, the stock market, along with most other investment options, lost massive amounts of its value over the course of weeks. What happened to real estate prices, you ask? Almost nothing. So, if you were in the stock market, you had to corner the market on Pepto-Bismol, and if you were in real estate, you didn't miss a beat. Real estate prices stayed constant as a new normal was found, and then they got back to what they normally do—go up. Real estate is the cruise ship of investments. It moves in one direction, and the market turns ever so slowly.

Consistent Appreciation

If you look at a chart of real estate home price growth, you see a consistent upward trend with no major downturns except the one that everyone loves to point out: 2008. The chart of home prices from the year 1900 to today shows a slow and steady climb in the price of homes until the big drop in 2008—after which the prices went back up again. In the next chapter we will get into the supply-and-demand side of real estate a lot more and talk specifically about what happened in 2008, but suffice it to say, a market is made up of two things, supply and demand. Real estate prices do go through corrections, but it happens slowly and usually in a very minimal amount before heading back up again. Over enough time real estate always appreciates.

A Natural Hedge Against Inflation

The chief measure of inflation we use in the United States is the CPI (Consumer Price Index). From 1965 to 2016 the total inflation as measured by the CPI was around 650 percent. The growth in the US median home price in that same period of time was over 1,200 percent.

If we follow those numbers further, there has been an even larger growth in home prices as inflation, post-pandemic, has set in. That natural hedging effect is to be expected, as the person who chooses to buy real estate has chosen it as an alternative to staying in dollars. In other words, if we know the value of the dollar is going to go down (due to inflation), we should get out of dollars into something else that people buy with those dollars. If the dollars become less valuable, people will simply need to give me more of them to buy the same piece of real estate.

To understand this, imagine you want to buy a car. The person selling the car does not want to accept cash; instead the seller will only accept stock with a value equal to the car's price in cash. You agree to trade some stock in order to purchase the car, and you find out that the particular company's shares that the seller will accept are trading at $50 per share. If the car is a $50,000 car, you would need to give the seller 1,000 shares. If the price of the stock fell to $25 per share, you would now need to give the seller 2,000 shares to buy the same car. The car has remained unchanged; only the value of what you are using to buy it with has changed.

The reason inflation makes real estate prices go up faster than normal is that real estate hasn't changed; only the money we are using to buy it has changed by becoming less valuable. Another way to think of this is to remember how much money a can of Coke cost from a vending machine when you were a kid. If you are in your mid-twenties or older, it was definitely cheaper. Has the Coke changed? The answer is no. We need more money to buy the exact same thing. If it takes more money to buy the same can of Coke, why wouldn't it take more money to buy the same house? Real estate protects us from inflation by allowing us to choose to get out of dollars and into something tangible that people need.

Tax Advantages

There are many tax advantages to real estate. They allow real estate buyers—whether they're living in a home they bought or they're property investors—to keep more of what they earn and to make money on their properties. While you are not a tax professional, it is important to understand the tax benefits your product brings to the table so you can make the customer aware of them. We will also look at the steps to figure out a ballpark for what these benefits would be for particular properties.

Let's start with folks planning to live there.

Tax-Free Profits

There are few places where you can make any money and Uncle Sam doesn't come a knocking to get a taste of the action. The government taxes you pretty much anytime you make any profit anywhere. That is except when you make a profit on the sale of your primary residence. Provided that you have lived there at least two of the last five years, you get an automatic exclusion to a big chunk of potential gain.

How big is that chunk? For an individual, you get to make a profit of $250,000 without paying any tax. If you are a married couple, you can double that deduction to $500,000. To be clear, that's a half a million dollar profit you can make without paying any taxes on it. Not a bad deal, huh?

How to Calculate Tax on Real Estate Profits

Step 1. Confirm the property qualifies (the primary resident has lived there two of the last five years).

Step 2. Find out the original purchase price plus any closing costs and add them together.

For example:

$385,000 + $15,000 = $400,000 total acquisition cost

Step 3. Find out the current sale price minus any closing costs. Sticking with our example:

$970,000 − $57,000 = $913,000 total sale proceeds

Step 4. Subtract the sale price from the original purchase price to get the profit:

$913,000 − $400,000 = $513,000

Step 5. Subtract the exclusion qualified for from the profit:

$513,000 − $500,000 married couple
exclusion = $13,000 taxable

If the owners had made improvements to the property, this would further reduce or eliminate their taxable income. This is something their accountant will be responsible for solving, but also something their real estate professional should know as it can affect when and if they should sell.

Tax Deduction for Mortgage Interest

Another very nice thing about real estate when it comes to taxes is that, regardless of whether you are living in the property or it is an investment, the interest portion of your mortgage payment is tax deductible. This means you can pay it with pretax dollars. This is a major difference when compared with someone who is renting. Renters must pay tax on their income, and then they can pay their rent out of what is left over.

How to Calculate the Tax Benefit of Owning Versus Renting

Step 1. What is the customers' top tax bracket? This is the discount they will receive on the dollars they save from the tax benefit until they transition to a lower bracket.

For this example, let's say their top bracket is 25 percent.

Step 2. How much do they earn?

Let's say $100,000.

Step 3. How much interest will they pay on their mortgage in year one?

Let's say $20,000.

Step 4. Subtract the mortgage interest from their income:

$$\$100,000 - \$20,000 = \$80,000 \text{ taxable income}$$

Step 5. Multiply the tax savings by the tax rate:

$$\$20,000 \times 25\% = \$5,000 \text{ tax savings}$$
$$\text{from buying versus renting}$$

Please note that this calculation is an oversimplification to give you the general idea how this works.

In the case of an investor, this tax deduction shields more of the received rental income from taxation and thus leaves more income available for the owner. To illustrate, if my investor's interest portion of the debt service (mortgage) payment is $30,000 annually and the property generated $80,000 in annual income, my investor would need to pay tax on $50,000 worth of income. The value of this becomes clearer when you realize that if the buyer purchased the property in cash, then the person would need to pay tax on all $80,000.

How to Calculate Taxable Income on a Rental Property

Step 1. Determine properties NOI (net operating income).
Let's say $80,000.

Step 2. Determine interest portion of the debt service (mortgage payment).

This can be gotten from an amortization schedule. Let's say $30,000.

Step 3. Subtract the mortgage interest payment from the NOI:
$80,000 − $30,000 = $50,000 in taxable income.

This is as opposed to our cash buyer who does not have this benefit and has to pay tax on all $80,000.

I know some folks may be saying, "Wait, the investor has more than just that deduction to reduce income. The investor should be paying on less income than that $50,000. That is because our investor gets the benefit of depreciation, which is our next topic.

Depreciation

This is an amazing tax benefit that is available to investors only. Depreciation is the opposite of appreciation. Appreciation is when something goes up in value; depreciation is when something goes down in value. This is easier to understand if we were to think about buying a car. Understand that, in order to buy the car, not only must you first earn the money to buy it, but you must earn enough to pay the full income taxes on the money you used to pay for it. Once you have done that, then you can actually make the purchase.

The IRS recognizes that you bought this car with money you paid taxes on and, over time, the car will be worth less and less, which means you have suffered a loss in value. Rather than making you sell the car to recognize the loss and then letting you deduct that from your tax bill, the IRS lets you take annual losses against the value of the car. The agency calls this depreciation. It lets you say that the car has so much usable life, and it will let you take a loss each year on your taxes for the portion of the usable life of the vehicle that has been used up.

If we bought a $50,000 car, we would need to pay tax on all $50,000 we earned to buy it. If the IRS said the car's usable life is five years, we would have a $10,000 tax deduction for the next five years to acknowledge the loss in value that we have suffered. This works because the car is truly losing value. The thing is, do real estate prices go up or down with time? I'll give you a hint—the answer is not down. So, if the price of real estate is going up, but I am still able to show a loss that reduces my taxable income, that is pretty freaking awesome.

The way this works for real estate is that it only applies to improved properties, not raw land. The IRS knows that dirt doesn't wear down or go down in value. Anything you add to the land though (like buildings, parking lots, swimming pools, lighting, etc.) is considered an "improvement" and will wear down with time, so that can be used to justify a loss. Basically, the IRS allows investors to take a loss against their taxable income for the loss in value they experience from the improvements wearing down.

Almost all real estate has a land component to it though, so how do we know how much to depreciate and how much we can't? We need to make what is called an "allocation." We need to determine how much of the property's value is land and how much is improvement. This is usually expressed in a percentage. So, say it was a $1 million property and the allocation was 80 percent improvement and 20 percent land; then we would have an $800,000 depreciable basis.

There are two magic numbers to remember for this: 27.5 and 39. For any residential investment property, regardless of size, the investor can depreciate the property over 27.5 years. If it is commercial nonresidential, it is depreciated over 39 years. That means with the above example, if it was residential, we would just divide our $800,000 depreciable basis by 27.5 and that would tell us how much of a loss we can take each year for the next 27.5 years.

How to Calculate Depreciation

Step 1. Figure out the allocation from land values, or get the information from your accountant:

A split of 80/20 is a very common one, so let's say 80 percent improvement and 20 percent land.

Step 2. Get your depreciable basis by multiplying purchase price by allocation:

$$\$1,000,000 \times 80\% = \$800,000$$

Step 3. Get your tax deduction. Divide the basis by the allowed period for the property:

$$\$800,000/27.5 \text{ (residential property)} = \$29,090$$

Step 4 (optional). Add to the mortgage interest tax deduction to show the investor total:

$$\$30,000 + 29,090 = \$59,090 \text{ total tax deduction}$$

Step 5 (optional). Subtract the total deduction from NOI to get the total taxable income:

$$\$80,000 - 59,090 = \$20,910 \text{ total taxable income}$$

Some folks feel like this is unfair and gives investors too much of an advantage. Remember, the money an investor uses to buy a car or a piece of property is money that taxes have been paid on already. This is just the investor getting a temporary rebate on taxes already paid. If you feel it's unfair, don't worry; the IRS wants the money back. When an investor sells the property, the IRS will charge a special tax called "recapture" (or "cost recovery") tax to the investor on the amount that the investor has depreciated and that is recovered with the sale. The reason this is still a benefit to the investor is twofold:

1. The investor had the use of the money that was saved in taxes to reinvest elsewhere.
2. There is a way to avoid having to pay that recapture tax.

Capital Gains

While capital gains is a tax, it's included here as a benefit because the rate is lower than what the investor pays on ordinary income. This means an investor would make more money by buying a property that appreciated by $10,000 per year than by getting a $10,000-a-year raise. As of the writing of this book, there were three capital gains rates: 0 percent (for those in the lowest income brackets), 15 percent (which almost everyone else pays), and 20 percent (only those in the highest ordinary income bracket pay this).

For each tax bracket, those rates are lower than what people pay on the money they make at their job. Lest you think this too is unfair, realize that the money initially invested was taxed, and that money has now been reinvested and the income earned on it is now being taxed. This exists to provide an incentive for people to invest.

How to Calculate Capital Gains Tax

Step 1. Add the original purchase price and the closing costs. For example:

$$\$1,000,000 + \$50,000 = \$1,050,000$$

Step 2. Add any capital improvements:

$$\$1,050,000 + \$100,000 = \$1,150,000$$

Step 3. Get current sale price minus closing costs:

$$\$1,500,000 - \$80,000 = \$1,420,000$$

Step 4. Subtract the current price from the total of step 2 to get your total capital gain:

$$\$1,420,000 - \$1,150,000 = \$270,000 \text{ in capital gain}$$

Step 5. Multiply by your capital gains rate to get how much tax you must pay:

$$\$270,000 \times 15\% = \$40,500 \ldots \text{ouch!}$$

1031 Exchange

This allows an investor to swap one piece of property for another one, without having to pay the taxes for the sale. This doesn't eliminate the taxes; it just "kicks the can down the road." The IRS allows the sale to be a nontaxable event. The investor is not allowed to ever touch the money though. A qualified intermediary is required to do this, and there is a time limit of 180 days from the date of sale to complete the new purchase. If the investor is not able to close on a new property in that time frame, the investor will owe all the tax from the sale. The investor must also disclose to the seller that they are buying the property as part of a 1031 exchange. This is a bit of a downside, as it lets any seller know that the buyer has time pressure—which can hurt the buyer's ability to negotiate.

The investor will also carry forward the depreciated basis from the last property so that the IRS can get its pound of flesh when the investor sells the new property—provided the investor doesn't do another 1031 exchange. How many of these can you do, you may ask? How many stars are there in the sky? You can do as many as you want. The deals need to make financial sense to do, as the intermediaries are not free. All in all though, this is a fabulous tool that our product has available for customers that makes real estate a really special investment type.

Cash Flow

With most other investments that offer passive growth, in order to receive any of the benefit of that growth, you have to sell some of your investment. If I owned stock and it went up in value, to take advantage of that increase, I would need to sell some stock. Not so with real estate. I can get rent money on a property without selling any portion of it.

Inexpensive to Finance

Borrowing money for the purposes of purchasing real estate is one of the lowest interest rate loans typically available. There are many reasons for this. First, strong title laws in the United States give lenders great certainty that if the loan defaults, they will be able to get free title to the property to sell and recover their loaned money. This is not the case in other parts of the world. As a result, in those countries loans are riskier, and the banks charge much higher rates if they will lend money at all.

Another reason why loans in the United States are relatively inexpensive is because of the stability of the real estate market and its long history of appreciation over time. A lender's greatest risk with a loan is in the very early stages, right after the loan is first made. The borrower has paid down very little principal, and there has been no real appreciation in the value of the property. As the borrower makes the payments, the borrower is reducing the amount owed to the bank and simultaneously the bank's risk. Also, as the property appreciates, it increases the value of the bank's collateral, which also reduces the bank's risk. This stability limits the bank's higher-risk window and allows for lower rates.

Long-Term Fixed-Rate Financing

The ability of borrowers to lock in an interest rate for the life of the loan gives them payment security. Not many other parts of life allow you to lock in a number today that you will pay for the next 30 years. This removes the risk of higher interest rates adversely affecting the buyer's ability to afford the payments.

Tangible

There is something special about an investment that you can see, touch, and taste (never let the customer taste the real estate without getting a lead-based paint disclosure signed first). For many investors, this tangibility is a major factor in their choosing real estate over investments such as stocks.

Utility

Shelter is one of the most basic human needs, right after food and water. People always need a place to live. They do not always need shares of stock. You can live in a house, not so much with a mutual fund. That utility means that an investment property could turn into an emergency residence if needed because it still functions to provide shelter.

One of the Greatest Wealth-Building Tools Ever Invented

One statistic I read said that nearly 90 percent of all businesses that exist in the United States today were started by one or more of the founders taking out equity against their primary home to fund the start of that business. That means the wealth that people built silently in their home is the reason why 9 out of 10 businesses we have today exist at all. That is crazy when you think about it. It also makes real estate the greatest wealth-building tool ever for middle-class people.

• • •

That covers all the pros of real estate that you must be able to articulate when working with customers. In the next chapter, we'll discuss the cons of buying and owning property—which are equally important for you to know.

CHAPTER 8

THE CONS OF REAL ESTATE (AND A FEW OTHER THINGS)

The advantages of real estate far outweigh the disadvantages, but there are situations where investing in real estate may not be the right decision for customers. As an agent, you need to understand both the pros and cons in order to help your customers make the best decision for their circumstances and goals.

To refresh your memory from the previous chapter, here are the cons of real estate:

- Lack of liquidity
- Tangible (it has problems too)
- Tenants (for investment properties)
- Repairs
- Leasing (for investment properties)
- Possibility of higher interest rates hurting buying power

THE CONS EXPLAINED

Here are a few of the disadvantages.

Lack of Liquidity

In investment classes I often ask, "How many people in this room are real estate investors?" Some hands go up, but many don't. I then ask, "How many of you real estate investors have ever been real estate rich and cash poor?," and nearly every investor hand goes back up. It is very easy in real estate to wind up in this position, primarily because it takes time to find a buyer and sell real estate. This is different from investments like stocks or mutual funds where it's usually simple to sell them. With real estate, there is a tangible asset that needs to be inspected; in addition, the title needs to be cleared, and the product needs to be priced without the benefit of a listed price a buyer will pay (as is the case with the stock market).

All of this means our real estate owner is looking at a minimum of about 15 days to get out of a property if the property is priced extremely low. More commonly, it will take close to 30–60 days. That doesn't seem like too much time until you find yourself short on cash. Having millions of dollars in real estate and no idea how to find the money to pay the light bill is an all too familiar experience for real estate investors. That delayed access to liquid capital has serious ramifications for how agents should advise their customers to invest. If you know your stuff, this offers a great opportunity to build both credibility and trust with your customers—which we will discuss in later chapters.

Tangible (It Has Problems Too)

How can this be both on the good list and on the bad list? Well, think about being married to a person who is a great cook. While you will get to enjoy delicious meals—a good thing—you very well may gain a bunch of weight—a bad thing.

In real estate, tangibility gives great confidence, but it leads to problems too. My tangible asset has tangible toilets that clog up and overflow at two in the morning, causing me to get my tangible backside out of my tangible bed (and interrupting a very nice, yet sadly intangible dream) to get the toilets fixed. My GE stock does not have this problem.

Tenants (for Investment Properties)

You can screen prospective tenants until you are blue in the face, but that is still no guarantee that your tenant will not become a huge pain in the butt. There are some professional tenants that make their way through life working the system and taking advantage of the laws designed to protect tenants. While getting one of these problem tenants is a nonzero risk, it is not super common either. It is just one more investment risk that needs to be accounted for and baked into the cake.

Repairs

Stuff breaks, and it costs money to fix. Investors all like making money, and spending money on repairs cuts into potential profits, particularly if the repairs are not planned for in advance. Repair costs cause the property's cash flow to be uneven and can be a real problem for investors who depend upon the income from their rental properties to survive. This uneven income is different from something like an annuity that has a stable payout. Typically, the rate of return on real estate will be higher, but that is because of the added risks associated with it.

Leasing (for Investment Properties)

Tenants pay rents, and rents are good. Acquiring tenants is not always free though. Often the acquisition of the people that provide your cash flow requires you to pay a commission or finder's fee. That reduces your income and lowers the overall rate of return.

Possibility of Higher Interest Rates Hurting Buying Power

Real estate markets are heavily affected by a change in interest rates. As rates go up, the hike functions as a price increase for the buyer who chooses to borrow money. Even if the purchase price stays the same, higher interest rates may make the property unaffordable for some buyers.

A FEW OTHER CONCEPTS YOU MUST KNOW

Here are a few other helpful concepts to make sure you know your stuff when talking about real estate with customers.

Why Homeowners Win

In the previous chapter, I gave an example of a $60,000 savings on a $325,000 purchase versus renting the same house for $2,550 per month. The reason our home purchaser made so much in just five years, even though the annual rent was lower than the annual mortgage payment and expenses, is because of two things:

1. The owner took the mortgage interest tax deduction (that we already discussed).
2. The home appreciated while the owner lived there.

That appreciation belongs 100 percent to the owner. Even if the owner put zero money down to buy the home and the property appreciated $100,000 in value, that $100,000 belongs to the owner and not the bank. In a typical market, real estate appreciation usually runs about 3–3½ percent per year.

Another thing working against the rental is the fact that rents tend to go up with time, while the mortgage payment for the homeowner stays fixed. This means each year the cost to live in the rental goes up, while the cost to live in the purchased property remains the same. So, the longer someone lives in a house, the better that differential will look.

When to Rent

One of the most important things to close customers for life is telling customers the truth. The above example makes it sound like buying a home is always better than renting it. That is not always the case. Sometimes renting is the superior option.

If you bought a home today and sold it tomorrow, it is pretty obvious that you would lose money on the deal because of the costs associated with buying and selling. These come out of the transaction and reduce how much you receive. In order for the purchase to make sense, the home must appreciate enough and you must benefit from the tax deduction for mortgage interest long enough to pay you back for the costs on the way in and out of the property.

So, the thing that determines when it starts to make sense to buy instead of rent is time. When is the tipping point, you may ask? It depends on the market. In a normal market, you need to hold the property two years or more for buying to be a better financial choice than renting.

Inflation

In a market with more inflation, rents and home prices tend to go up more quickly. Home prices in the last inflationary cycle of the 1970s averaged more than 9 percent growth per year, and rents averaged 8 percent increases. So, renters experienced the worst of both worlds. Their rent increased a lot. And at the same time, the prices of houses they might want to buy became more expensive. The customers that chose to purchase, on the other hand, just see the value of their home continue to increase. There is a line in real estate that I love:

> What is the difference between experiencing inflation and
> appreciation?
>   Ownership.

Inflation and Wages

One of the important things to know about inflationary times is that wages tend to go up faster than normal, but they do not go up fast enough to keep pace with the devaluation of the money. This means that the owners have a fixed housing expense that allows them to build more wealth during inflationary times, whereas renters have to watch their standard of living fall, as 100 percent of their expenses increase with inflation.

Cap Rate

Comparing real estate deals with each other is an important part of working with investors. Investors have a vast array of choices of what to do with their money. A good agent helps them to choose the best available option for them. To do this you need to know how to evaluate the options.

The fastest and easiest way to compare options is to calculate the capitalization rate (cap rate) for each investment. To find the cap rate, you need to find out how much income a property earns after all expenses are paid and then divide that net operating income by the purchase price of the property. This will give you a percentage, which represents what each dollar in the investment is earning for you. For example, if you had an NOI of $10,000 and a purchase price of $100,000, you would have a rate of return of 0.10, which is 10 percent. That means every dollar you invest is earning you 10 cents per year if the rents and expenses stay the same.

Beyond Cap Rate

Another basic principle that as a real estate professional you should be aware of is the two ways investors make money in real estate. The first way is the increase in the value of the property over time, which is called "appreciation." The second way investors make money is by investing in an income-producing property and raising rents over time.

When investors buy a piece of income-producing real estate, what they are doing is exchanging money today for the right to the property's future cash flows and the future sale price of the property. This means the full value of an income property can't be calculated unless rent increases and future appreciation are calculated into the equation.

According to that measure, the capitalization rate I just showed you is deficient because it doesn't consider either of those things. A cap rate is a good tool for comparing similar pieces of real estate that are likely to appreciate at about the same rate and that are likely to support similar rent increases. So, in those cases, we don't need to bother considering other factors. We can just compare the current income with the purchase price to figure out which is the best deal. This is like playing a board game with your friend. If at the end of the game you both score a bonus 20 points, and you are the only two people playing, and you agree to not count those extra points, the winner of the game and margin of victory will be completely unaffected.

An App You Want to Have

A good financial calculator is very helpful to show customers that you know what you are talking about. You want a calculator that specializes in compounding interest over time. That is very important in real estate because you need it to determine your customers' mortgage payments, calculate investor returns, project future rents, project a future sale price of a property, and let sellers know how much they will owe the bank at closing if they give you the listing and you sell the home.

There are some great financial apps that you can download on your phone. This is great because you always have your phone with you. The one that I use is the HP 10bii. Investing the time and effort to learn to use this tool has proved to be the best thing I could do in building my confidence in speaking with even the most financially knowledgeable customers.

Staying on Top of the News

Let's stick with the tech theme for a bit. As I've discussed, there are many things in the world that affect the real estate market. Staying on top of those things is something a real estate professional should do. Many agents don't like to read books or look for articles, as it gets in the way of the really important things in life—like posting cat videos on Facebook (I mean social media marketing). For many people, keeping up with the business news is miserable, as they just don't know where to even start. Here is the solution:

Step 1. Download a business news app.

Step 2. Don't open it.

Step 3. Turn on the push notifications so it sends you only the important stories.

Step 4. Read them.

Step 5. Ask yourself, how would that affect real estate?

We will talk about what stories to pay attention to most in the next chapter. Having this tool gives you a way to be relevant and develop an informed opinion based on current events.

Where and How You Work

This may seem a bit outside the scope of the topics we have been covering, but I really wish people had told me this stuff when I started. I had to figure all this out by trial and error. Eventually, I figured out where and how to set up my base of operations to get the best results. These are not rules, but suggestions that have helped me improve my productivity and reduce my discomfort. So, let me serve as your guinea pig. Please learn from my mistakes and avoid making the same ones yourself.

First, in our business we spend a lot of time sitting. There are standing desks and treadmill desks, but for most of us our bottom is where we spend a lot of our time. Since that's the case, invest in a comfortable chair with good lower back support.

When it comes to your computer, make sure your monitors are eye level or a bit higher. We spend too much time looking down because of our addiction to our cell phones. This is screwing up all our necks and doing a great job of keeping the chiropractic trade alive and thriving. By getting your monitors mounted so that when you are looking straight ahead you are looking at the bottom third of the monitor, you are setting up a workstation to help reinforce good posture and keep you healthy and pain-free at work. Your CEO needs to keep the staff healthy to maximize what they can achieve.

Also, talking about monitors, the more the merrier. I have found three monitors to be the ideal number to use to get stuff done. Having one monitor dedicated to email helps keep you on top of all incoming info and sets you up to have a reputation of being a responsive person to work with. That does require you to actually respond to those incoming emails when you see them. That dedicated monitor for email lets you manage your virtual mailbox more effectively.

Here is my last and most painful suggestion for where and how you work: Be organized. There are two places in particular where that needs to happen. First, your CRM (customer relationship management) needs to be up to date with an active task for every customer. Second, you want to have an email inbox with zero emails in it. Email is where news comes that you often must react to in a time-sensitive way. If your inbox is cluttered, it becomes easier to miss stuff. Missing stuff should not be part of your business standards, right?

Saying "I read most important emails" is like saying "I dodge most incoming bullets." It only takes one screwup, and you have a big problem. Also, attending to all your emails makes record keeping much easier if there is some kind of dispute or if there is ever a threat of litigation. If you have great records, that tends to cool legal threats down really quick, provided of course that you did quality work. Detailed records of a screwup are not quite as helpful. If you want to avoid missing things or the time wasted searching for emails, then maybe your CEO should empower the staff to do what's necessary to make sure every email is read, responded to in an appropriate manner, and stored in an easy-to-find place.

Having an efficient and comfortable place to work sets your staff up to enjoy going to work and getting stuff done while you are there. That sounds like you are a CEO who is actually doing your job, doesn't it? If you want happy customers, having happy employees can't hurt. Having efficient employees who get work done quickly and are very responsive puts your business among the absolute elite of the real estate industry. Customers and our industry are desperate for professionals who work like that. This means there is a strong demand for this type of professionalism. Will *you* do what *you* need *you* to do to meet that demand? Part of what knowing your stuff entails is knowing how to get the best out of yourself.

THREE AREAS THAT NEED FOCUS

There are three major areas to which agents don't typically allocate enough time to become proficient. These are topics I teach extensively. In fact, every time I think I have written all there is on these topics, I recognize a different facet of them and have to write more. These are the areas that really have the ability to separate what you know from what your competitors know. They include the investment of real estate, negotiation, and valuation.

The Investment of Real Estate

We touched on a little bit of this earlier in this chapter and will do so more in the next, because this is one of the most important things most agents don't focus on—and this is to their detriment. It is a giant topic and the one I have written more classes on than anything else. Every time you ask a customer to buy a property, you're asking that customer to make an investment. Every time.

Your ability to understand, explain, and compare the purchase with financial alternatives is a true game changer. Investors need to know what the best thing is to do. If you can't show them and you are supposed to be their real estate expert, then who the heck is going to do that? The customer? I thought you wanted to be respected and treated like a professional? Do you want the customer to know your job better than you and still treat you like an expert? If you possess the skills to analyze and compare different investments, three things happen:

1. You are perceived as a much better asset by your customer.
2. You actually know how to do your business.
3. You help someone make the best decision possible based on objective data.

Negotiation

This is a critical skill in this business. You don't just negotiate with the other side; you also have to negotiate with your customer. And don't forget about the toughest of all negotiations: the negotiations we have with ourselves.

Most negotiation training available in real estate is built upon fostering collaborative negotiations. This is definitely something that you should learn, as collaborative negotiations are the best kind if they are possible. Both parties are trying to find things to make the pie bigger so that they feel like everyone is getting a good deal. Both parties tend to walk away happier and get more of what they value. The issue that exists in real estate is the myopic focus on this type of negotiation. For this type of negotiation to occur, I need to have a collaborative negotiator on the other side. As it turns out, that doesn't happen all the time, and I can't control when it does. I can always be open to it and try to drive things that way, but at the end of the day, "it takes two to tango."

When it is not a collaborative negotiation, we have what is called a "competitive negotiation." This type of negotiation is built around the idea that there is only so much pie, pie is delicious, and therefore I want as much of this pie for me and my side as I can get and I don't care how little you get stuck with. This type of negotiation is loaded with tricks and tactics that are not taught in most negotiation classes that I have attended. As an agent, your job is to protect and defend your customers' position. If you are not prepared to do that, then you are not prepared to be their agent. Even if you don't like to use the tactics, you need to learn to recognize them when they are being done to you. Calling them out when people use these things on you is a great way to lessen their ability to affect the negotiation.

I am a firm believer that to be a good agent, you need to be able to be tough when it is called for. Bolstering your negotiation game by learning the ways to be as compelling as possible, and using the best tools and tactics to do so, should be part of any agent's path to achieving mastery and building a business to be proud of.

Valuation

Knowing what things are worth is very important for agents, especially if they are trying to build a listing business. Customers always want to know what things are worth. The person that is often the true final arbiter of what a property is worth is the appraiser. Only in a cash deal or in a market where buyers are paying over the appraised value is this not the case. So, if appraisers determine what things are worth, and we want to have values that hold up, maybe we should look to see how they do their values. Appraisers have a standardized set of guidelines for doing their valuations, known as the USPAP (Uniform Standards of Professional Appraisal Practice).

There are three methods of valuation that are used in real estate:

1. **Replacement cost.** The least commonly used valuation approach, replacement cost identifies what the cost to rebuild the building plus land cost minus depreciation would be.

2. **Income approach.** This method looks at the income a property generates and what cap rate investors are willing to accept in the area. To get the market value of the property, divide the NOI by the cap rate to determine what the property is worth.

3. **Comparable method.** For most residential real estate transactions, the comparable method is used, except in very unusual circumstances. This approach looks at similar properties that have sold and compares them with the property being valued. The property being valued is called the "subject property," and the properties that have sold or are active listings are called the "comparable properties."

The thing is, not all properties are the same. The most important criteria to make sure the properties are similar are proximity (in the same or close to the same neighborhood); time (the more recent the sale of a comparable property, the less likely the market has changed in the interim); and size (is it close to the same size of other properties that have sold?).

Typically, appraisers will want closed sales from the past six months (and preferably three months). In an urban area, the comparable properties should be within one-half mile of the subject (one-quarter mile is preferred), and within 20 percent of the size of the subject property (the closer in size, the better).

There are many more things that appraisers look at in valuing a house. The real work of getting a valuation right involves making adjustments for things like an extra bedroom, an extra bathroom, a pool, a garage, or anything else that is different. Sometimes the homes are similar in size, but one was built 50 years ago, and the subject is new construction. All these things require the agent, who is trying to anticipate what the appraised value will be, to know what these things are worth in the area the property is located. This knowledge can be found by paying attention to what things sell for in your MLS. That is where the appraisers go for the majority of their information. Most agents have access to this, but they just don't take advantage of it. Use it to educate yourself on how differences in properties impact valuations. You especially want to focus on this in your farm area.

· · ·

OK, this is a lot of stuff. But that's good. Look at it this way: Building your knowledge and understanding confirms to the customers that they need a real estate professional to help them navigate these issues. So, that's job security for you.

There is more to learn though. Until now, we've mostly discussed general things you must know about your product. However, your product is part of the market, and that means your expertise needs to extend beyond just the product and to the economics that govern how your product behaves.

CHAPTER 9

WHY YOU NEED TO KNOW YOUR REAL ESTATE HISTORY

My dad used to tell me that you need to know where you are and where you want to go if you have any hope of getting there. An example he gave of this was in retail. One day out of the blue he asked me this question: "If you have a product and you discount it 20 percent to increase sales and then you decide it's time to end the sale, wouldn't you just increase the price 20 percent to go back to where you started"?

I knew better than to weigh in on this, as I knew the answer would be forthcoming and I would probably get it wrong. He said, "Many businesses have gone out of business by getting this wrong. If you have a $100 item and discount it 20 percent, it is now an $80 item. If you then increase it 20 percent, it doesn't go back to $100 because 20 percent of $80 is only $16. That means you are selling the item for only $96 instead of your goal to sell it at the original price. Fortunes have been lost on the back of these simple mistakes."

So, in this case, failing to recognize where the price was and what you were trying to accomplish with the price increase led to missing the actual destination. This same idea applies but looks very different in real estate. Here's an example.

A customer came to me wanting to invest. She wanted to buy a condo near the beach where she could live six months of the year and rent it out for the other six. I immediately tried to talk her out of making this poor business decision. Why was it so bad? Because there are two competing ideas at play. If you're living somewhere, you'll be tempted to purchase those $30,000 Tibetan marble countertops that you fell in love with and just *have* to have. Meanwhile, if you're buying countertops for an investment property, you would probably spend a fraction of that amount for the tenant to be comfortable. Doing anything else increases the amount of your investment without increasing the income in a meaningful way and thus destroys your rate of return.

The savings from not staying at hotels by living in the property for six months a year would not be worth the long-term damage to the investment's performance. I know there are short-term rental folks out there reading this whose heads are about to explode. But this customer was not interested in entering the hotel business, and so this model was not on the table. It is possible to do a hybrid investment/personal vacation rental, but personal use should not drive that investment decision.

You must keep the destination in sight. This customer came to me wanting to invest in a long-term rental property. That was the goal. By keeping that in mind, I helped her understand why it made more sense to buy a triplex. With three rental units, she would reduce her vacancy risk. Even if one unit wasn't rented, the others probably would be. We found a property that was performing relatively well in the market, getting about a 6.5 percent rate of return.

The appraiser's valuation of the property was about $60,000 below what we had offered. In the last chapter, we talked about how important it is to understand valuations and get them right. Here is why it matters. When I took a look at his calculations, I realized that he was comparing the triplex against three different three-bedroom, two-bathroom, single-family homes of a similar size in the area. The issue is that one is a multifamily income property and the others are single-family homes that would be lived in full-time. Two very different types of properties—they needed to be valued differently.

I contested the appraisal and even got an apology from the banker, and the bank offered to order an alternate appraisal. Ultimately, my customer decided she wanted to move forward quickly and agreed to pay the difference; she liked the property and trusted my judgment. Now, not even a year later, her rate of return on that property is close to 11 percent because the rent growth I had projected due to the inflationary market at the time occurred.

Surveys show that the main reason customers choose to work with an agent is because they're terrified of making a mistake. In the example above, by understanding the economics of the market, I saved my client from making the wrong decision. I demonstrated the value I could bring to the table, gave her a sense of peace about the property she was purchasing, and closed her as a customer for life.

In my father's example at the beginning of this chapter, he stressed why you need to pay attention to discounting percentages in the retail business. In real estate, you need to pay attention to your market and the economics that underpin it.

KNOW YOUR HISTORY

One of the biggest tools that agents have at their disposal but are never taught about is the history of real estate. When I invest in cryptocurrencies, I have no idea what to expect because there is a very limited history with them to review. I don't know how they will react to an oil shortage, attempts at regulation, inflation, or the Federal Reserve raising interest rates. With real estate, I don't have that problem because we have seen how real estate behaves in face of all these factors before. I don't have to guess. Learning to use current events along with the history of our product to speak intelligently about where you think the product is headed is what a great agent should do. The trick is to know your history well enough so that you can show customers how the current market aligns or doesn't with previous markets.

During the time I wrote this chapter, in late 2022, customers commented all the time about how the market was in a huge bubble and real estate prices were going to tank. They often said the market they were experiencing was just like the one in 2008.

As an agent, you need to know not just what happened, but why it happened. This will allow you to assess if the same instigating causes exist in the current market. If the underlying conditions are different in the current market, then it is not reasonable to think the market will behave in the same way as it did before. However, if the same things that caused a previous market to crash exist in the current market, then it just makes sense that real estate will behave now as it did then.

To look at this deeply, I could discuss supply and demand, as well as economic theories on how markets operate. It probably would become complex and a little dry. I think it will be more fun to write about all this in down-to-earth terms that reflect everyday conversations about the market and the economy. If you've been in business any length of time, you probably already have a good understanding of how the economy works.

THE 2008 BUBBLE VERSUS
THE POST-PANDEMIC MARKET

So, let's address that elephant in the room right now. In 2008, we had a crisis that caused a major downturn in home prices. I like to quiz the agents in my classes about the causes of the 2008 crash. I ask, "Was it a supply-side issue or a demand-side issue?" Agents will say in response that the crash was caused by all the bad loans that banks made. I tell them that is a perfectly fine answer for a taxicab driver to give, but it is not a great answer for a real estate market expert to offer.

I then ask, "Who here wants to be perceived by the customer as a real estate market expert?" Almost every hand in the room goes up. I then follow up with, "Who here markets themselves currently like they are a real estate market expert?" Almost every hand goes up. "Yet the answer you gave is not a real estate market expert type of answer. Do you see why the customer might be confused?"

As market experts, we need to recognize that what led to the 2008 crash was a change in the long-held lending standards that had produced an incredibly stable real estate market for many previous decades. Lenders had settled on a lending criterion that allowed for the vast majority of loans to get fully repaid while still having enough risk in the portfolio for a reasonable number of foreclosures to exist. (If there were no foreclosures, it would indicate that the lending policy was too strict, and many folks who could take a loan and successfully pay it back were being denied because of lenders being too strict.)

In the late 1990s, lenders decided, with the government's encouragement, to start rolling back their lending criteria. So, they started making riskier and riskier loans. The model they used to justify making these loans was the fact that real estate home prices had never really gone down in a meaningful way in recent decades. So, rather than basing their lending decisions on the ability of borrowers to repay their loans, they started making loans based on the supposition that real estate prices would continue to go up.

The argument at the time was that the lending practices were too restrictive and thus deprived potential home ownership to people who should have the opportunity to own a home. By changing the lending criteria to focus more on the price appreciation of real estate, more people were able to buy homes. Naturally, this caused an increase on the demand side. I refer to these buyers who would not have previously qualified under the normal lender underwriting criteria as "artificial demand." When that artificial demand was added to the existing demand, then lo and behold, overall demand increased, and the supply became insufficient to meet that demand. As result, we experienced scarcity, and that (as always) made prices go up.

So, as naturally as night follows day, the increase in demand for houses in the early 2000s caused prices to rise rapidly. This incentivized the supply side (builders) to supplement the supply (build more freaking houses), but they couldn't keep up with the demand because lenders continued to lower their lending criteria, which further increased the demand and drove prices even higher.

The issue set in when lenders realized in late 2007 that many of the riskier loans they made to less creditworthy borrowers were not getting paid back at the same rate as traditionally underwritten loans from the past did. Lenders didn't see this coming for a long time—but once they did, they reacted strongly.

This is the part that makes 2008 so different from anything before. All at once, lenders saw they had a massive financial exposure, and overnight, banks all stopped making loans. They didn't go back to the solid underwriting criteria they had used for decades. They went to complete austerity by making almost no loans at all. The only person they would make a loan to at that time was the person who did not need one.

They went to this strict underwriting criterion to try to preserve their liquidity to weather what they could see would be an avalanche of loan defaults in the near future. This meant that no one could borrow money to buy a home, which removed almost all buyers from the market. And those that could still buy, without borrowing, stopped buying as well in order to wait and see where things were going. Overnight, the market went from an excess of demand to an extreme oversupply. This is something that we had never seen in real estate before.

When there is too much supply of any product, including houses, prices must come down to attract buyers. That is where the problem got worse though. The loans the banks made that were still performing after the initial wave of defaults were still based on the assumption that real estate prices would continue to go up. When those prices went down, the borrowers with these loans were no longer incentivized to stay in their homes. In fact, the upside-down situation (owing more on the property than the market value) many borrowers found themselves provided a strong disincentive to pay the mortgage on the property. These otherwise "good mortgages" then went into default. Those defaults became either foreclosures, short sales, or modifications.

The problem with loan modifications is that if the banks made deals to modify too sweet, even folks that didn't need help would seek a modification to get better terms. So, this meant that the banks had to keep the process and terms to get a modification difficult to avoid borrowers that could still pay their mortgages from exploiting the system. However, that commitment that banks had to draconian terms in their modification programs made it very hard for borrowers to pay back on their modified loan agreements—they simply weren't modified enough to make much of a difference to borrowers. As a result, borrowers who successfully modified their loans defaulted on those modifications at a rate of over 90 percent within the first year.

The other two options that banks had to eliminate the bad loans, short sales and foreclosures, had one thing in common—they both added inventory to the market, which was the last thing that an already oversupplied market needed.

As a result, following the 2008 crash, the market remained in oversupply for several years. The market needed to find a price point that would encourage people to buy up the existing inventory, but throughout that time more properties kept entering the market, putting downward pressure on prices and leading many buyers to postpone purchases in hopes of lower prices in the future.

Because both the foreclosure and short sale processes are fairly time consuming, the entrance of this extra supply was spread out over time. This was good and bad. It was good because it didn't swamp an already oversaturated market with a new glut of properties, but it was bad because it extended the length of time that the oversupply state lingered and why the recovery took so long.

HOW'S THE MARKET DOING?

What is the number one question people ask you when they find out you are in real estate? "How's the market?," right? Here's a crazy idea, since we know that we'll be asked that question repeatedly. Why don't we prepare to answer it right now? That way when we do get asked, we don't have to do the standard real estate move of channeling our inner Tony the Tiger and saying something really compelling like, "It's great!" And then moving on because that is all we had ready to say on that topic. Prepping to crush that question every single time will force you to pay attention to what's going on in the economy and the market. Knowing that information will always make you a better agent. Period.

Seeing as there is no way for me to know when you are reading this, let me compare the economics of the post-Covid market (when I was writing this book) with the housing bubble and burst of the early 2000s.

During the pandemic, decisions were made to close the economy to attempt to reduce the mortality of the virus. Whether you agreed with that policy or not, that is what happened, and that choice had major economic consequences. Fearing a severe economic slowdown, the Federal Reserve decided to print more money.

Here's what the government was so afraid of: Basically, if you stop the economy, businesses can't pay their employees. In turn those employees (and business owners) can't earn money to pay their mortgages, banks can't pay interest to their investors, and the investors can't fund more loans. Also, if businesses can't run, they can't pay their rent. If they can't pay their rent, their landlords won't have the money to pay their mortgages. If the landlords can't pay their mortgages, properties go into default and need to be foreclosed on. When enough of that happens and banks go into jeopardy of failing, that hurts their investors (like your grandma's pension fund), and credit lines throughout the economy dry up.

The worst-case scenario? A depression, massive unemployment, and social unrest. Not a good scenario for anyone—including politicians who want to get reelected.

So, to ensure that the money kept flowing through the economy and to prevent a possible depression, the government began a massive printing of money. Some estimates put the increase in the money supply going from $4 trillion in 2020 to as high as almost $20 trillion by 2022.

To understand how this big increase in money supply affected the value of money, we need to establish that the value of money in 2020 was based upon how much there was at the time compared with the demand. If we increase the supply of money five times, what do you think would be the normal response? The value of that money would go down.

Maybe the easiest way to think about this is to imagine there are 5 houses available and 10 buyers. We would expect there to be fierce bidding for those homes, as there are more buyers than homes. Now imagine someone adds 20 additional homes to the market. Now we have 25 available homes and only 10 buyers. The scarcity of homes has been reduced. When scarcity is reduced, prices will always fall. That is what happened to our dollars; they became less scarce, and their value fell faster than normal.

Typically, a 1½–3 percent inflation range is what we have come to expect since the late 1980s. Many people had never seen inflation much higher than that in their lifetime—but there are many instances in the past where inflation rose to double digits (and even triple digits in other countries).

By studying inflationary markets in history, we can see how real estate prices reacted back then and perhaps gain insight into what real estate prices were likely to do in the post-pandemic inflationary outbreak.

When I wrote this chapter, the rate of inflation was hovering around 9 percent, according to the Consumer Price Index. In the early to mid-2000s, that number was around 2–3 percent. The only thing really going up in price during that time was home prices. In contrast, in the post-Covid market, the price of everything was going up. Is that different? Well, yes. If the price of everything is going up, it indicates the value of money is the thing declining. If the price of only one thing is going up (as was the case of real estate in the early 2000s), it indicates either a shortage or a potential bubble.

Did these two markets differ? Yes, very much—but that was no guarantee that the banks wouldn't start lending like crazy again and crash the market like they did in 2008. That is a true statement.

So, during this time, I decided to investigate what banks were doing. According to the average of lenders I spoke to nationwide, the odds of a first-time mortgage applicant getting approved for a loan in 2022 was about 35 percent. In 2006 and 2007, that number was north of 95 percent. Basically, if you could fog up a mirror in 2007, you would get a loan, and if you couldn't, they had a guy that would come in and fog it up for you. This meant that banks in 2022 were turning down nearly two out of every three buyers and were thus being much more cautious with their lending than in the days leading up to the housing collapse of 2008. So, that indicated to me that banks had learned their lesson and had not created an environment that would require them to stop lending the way they did in 2008.

RESPONDING TO CUSTOMERS WITH FACTS

By focusing on facts, I was able to respond effectively to customers in 2022 who thought the market was going to drop significantly like it did during the 2008 housing crisis.

I began by pointing out that for prices to drop significantly, an oversupply of houses would have to develop. Again, at the time I wrote this chapter, every indicator of inventory levels showed the lowest inventory in decades. That meant we were in an undersupplied market.

There are three places inventory can come from: builders building more houses, more foreclosures coming onto the market, and more houses for sale. Let's look at all three in the 2022 marketplace:

1. **Builders.** Following the pandemic, builders were hesitant to build due to rising interest rates. It wasn't just the reduction in home loans impacting housing demand; builders were also hit by higher rates on their lines of credit. Higher interest rates made it more expensive for them to build homes. Those higher interest rates existed to combat the high inflation that was in the economy. With money less stable, builders were more cautious. Also, the uncertainty in supply chains increased the time to complete projects, which meant builders would take longer to complete and sell

homes. More time equals more interest payments, insurance, utilities, wear and tear, etc.—and all those costs eat into profits. This reduces the incentive for builders to produce new homes.

2. **Foreclosures.** Some people who believed a crash was coming thought there would be a wave of foreclosures. The problem with that logic is that the people who were losing their home had to be incentivized not to sell it and pay the bank back what remained on their loan. That's what happened in the 2008 housing crisis, because home values fell so much that the vast majority of loans were in a negative equity state, with people owing more on their loans than their houses were worth. In 2022, that was not the case. People had more equity, and everyone's homes had appreciated significantly post-Covid. That meant homeowners were incentivized to pay their mortgages or to sell their properties at a profit. So, that ruled out foreclosures as a big source of inventory that would have led to an oversupplied market.

3. **Listings.** An increase in listings occurs when people decide to sell and not rebuy. If people sell and rebuy, the market experiences a net zero inventory change. They add a unit in one place and reduce inventory in another by one. There are situations where people sell a home and do not rebuy. They may become renters, die, enter a retirement home, etc. But we would need a wave of these listings to change the current undersupply. As I write this, that doesn't seem to be a viable source of new supply either.

If none of these events were likely to occur, that meant we could not get to an oversupply state from the supply side. There was another way: the demand side. If we could reduce the demand enough so that there were fewer buyers than there were homes for sale then, boom, prices would start falling, and market crash here we come!

Of course, this would require a mass exodus of buyers from the market. What could cause this? The only obvious thing would be higher interest rates. Do people walk away in mass from higher interest rates? The answer is . . . I'm pausing for dramatic effect . . . no!

People do not leave the real estate market in mass—they do it slowly. First, it is true that higher interest rates increase the cost of borrowing and thus put a downward pressure on home prices. If that was the only factor affecting home prices, then the prices would definitely need to fall. However, higher interest rates do not occur in a vacuum; they signal to landlords that their tenants' alternative to renting just got more expensive. This allows the landlords to be more aggressive with pricing their rentals, which means rents rise more quickly. Higher rents incentivize people to stop renting and to buy their own home instead; that, of course, puts upward pressure on home demand, and by extension home prices.

Luckily though, you don't have to take my word for it because, back to the history we were discussing before, there is a much better correlation with another time in real estate history. The last major inflationary market that real estate went through was the 1970s. The average annual inflation rate was 7.25 percent. That doesn't seem too bad, right? The total inflation for the decade was 103.45 percent. This meant your 1970 dollar couldn't buy 50 cents worth of stuff by 1979. Interest rates were in the mid-7 percent range in 1970. By 1980, they were over 16 percent. When did real estate prices go down? The answer is they didn't. Table 9.1 charts some basic research of the history of home prices and interest rates.

Table 9.1   Home Prices and Interest Rates

Year	Interest	Average Home	% of Change
1970	7.50%	$17,000.00	
1980	16.63%	$47,200.00	177.6
1990	10.13%	$70,100.00	67.6
2000	8.05%	$119,600.00	51.2

Sources: https://www.cnbc.com/2017/06/23/how-much-housing-prices-have-risen-since-1940.html; https://inflationdata.com/Inflation/Inflation/DecadeInflation.asp.

To be clear, not only did home prices not fall; they actually increased at a faster rate than inflation. From 1970 to 1980, the rate of inflation ran 103.45 percent, and median home prices rose 177.6 percent. That is a 70 percent outperformance by the real estate. Would you get out of bed in the morning to go make a 70 percent rate of return on your money? Guess what—I bet your customers would too if some agent would just tell them what's going on.

What we just did here is compare various facets of the real estate market at a point in time with another market at a different point in time. The comparison shows that the market of 2008 does not corollate on the economic side to the 2022 market. Inflation was much lower in 2008 than it was in 2022. Also, there was no rapid expansion of buyers on the demand side due to banks making bad loans in 2022. Finally, there didn't appear to exist any inclination on the part of banks to cease lending and stop the market.

Given all these differences between 2008 and 2022, it didn't make sense to compare the two in hopes of predicting the future. Instead, the inflationary market of the 1970s was a better fit. The one major difference was that the tremendous amount of building that went on in the 1970s was not present in 2022. This meant that the supply was not getting added to as quickly, which meant that the scarcity of real estate would likely worsen and prices should continue to rise, especially as rents go up.

How do you feel about your product now? Was any of that super complicated? Was that boring information to take in? If you are interested in doing what's best for your customer, it shouldn't be.

The lesson of this chapter is to learn your real estate history and stay abreast with what's going on in the economy and the real estate market. You need to know your stuff. That means recognizing the market we're in now and how it relates to similar market conditions from the past.

Developing this expertise will enable you to get a leg up in speaking to customers in an interesting and engaging way and helping them to make better decisions.

CHAPTER 10

WHAT YOU NEED TO KNOW ABOUT ECONOMICS

One of the things that is not discussed much among agents is the economic factors that drive real estate. If we understand the connections between the economy and real estate, we'll know what to look for in the news, and it will be easier to stay on top of the things that drive the industry. Here are a few.

INTEREST RATES

Interest rates are the one part of the economy that people do talk about in the industry, probably because the rates directly affect home affordability. Because interest rates have such a direct impact on closing a deal, mortgage brokers and agents love to get on this topic.

But while agents talk about interest rates a lot, most don't even know where the rates come from, so they need to wait for mortgage brokers to tell them, "Hey, the rates went up." That's not great if you're purporting to be a real estate market expert. As mentioned earlier, the yield on the 10-year Treasury note is where the mortgage interest rates come from.

Not only do you want to pay attention to the current yield on 10-year Treasury notes, but you should also look for stories that discuss the things affecting yields and whether the rates are likely to go up or down in the future. If you as an agent have good reasons to believe that rates are going to go up or down, would that affect the advice you would give to customers? If the outlook is for rates to go down, might I encourage buyers to start looking now—but to slow down their selection process or make an offer with a little longer closing period? If the opposite is the case and rates are projected to increase, might I encourage sellers to get their property on the market sooner rather than later to take advantage of the fact that their property will be more affordable to buyers prior to the rate hike?

WAGES

Wages are another economic factor that impacts real estate. Around 80 percent of homes that are purchased use a mortgage to buy that home. One of the first questions a mortgage broker asks buyers is how much money they make, because that directly affects how much the buyers can pay for a house. When wages go up, the buyers can afford higher mortgage payments. If buyers can afford higher payments, guess what always happens to home prices? They go up.

So, if I want to build evidence that we are not in a bubble market, I need to see that wages are going up. If they are, then higher home prices are to be expected, and they are not indicative of a bubble.

Wages are released monthly by the Bureau of Labor Statistics and are reported as a percentage of growth. This brings up a sad but interesting phenomenon of how wages interact with our next item, inflation.

INFLATION

Inflation, as we have discussed, is the value of money going down. As the value of money goes down, wages tend to go up. The problem is that wages tend not to go up as quickly as the value of money goes down. In fact, for the last several decades, wages have lagged behind inflation for all but a couple of years. This means effectively that everybody is earning more money, but that money buys less stuff. In other words, everyone's standard of living is getting slightly squeezed, but it's happening slowly enough that we don't realize it. What helps minimize this is the fact that technology and innovation help to reduce the cost of things as well.

Keeping a handle on inflation can be a little trickier than other economic indicators because there are multiple ways to measure it.

THE CONSUMER PRICE INDEX

The most widely quoted inflation measure, which we mentioned earlier, is the Consumer Price Index, or CPI. The CPI consists of a basket of commonly purchased goods and compares the cost to buy that basket of goods today with what it cost last year. This would seem to be a pretty decent way to measure the variance in the buying power of money. However, there are a couple of caveats. One is that the CPI includes goods like oil and food that are often affected by outside market forces, and thus may give a false reading on the value of money. In other words, the price rise might be temporary. This becomes obvious if you think of a time of war. The price of oil might spike at this time, even though it is not really a reflection of the money being less valuable, only a change in the overall world market for oil.

The other big issue with the CPI is that it tends to consistently understate inflation due to it being too heavily weighted toward technology items. If there was a DVD player in the basket of goods in 1990, buying that DVD player back then might have meant selling some of your organs and perhaps your firstborn child. Today, that DVD player is so cheap that if you pay for the deluxe wax at the car wash, they will throw one in.

This natural change of technology items getting cheaper makes it look like the dollar gained buying power, which is typically not the case. So, the CPI tends to understate inflation—which politicians like because it makes them seem less inept. The understatement of inflation in the CPI isn't as big a problem as it may seem if we use it in the right way—as a relative number. How much more or less is the CPI from last month or last year? That comparison gives you a good solid number to base your opinion upon that is tough for a customer to dispute. The CPI comes out monthly, and it is a critical number to monitor. Nothing matters more to real estate (after interest rates) than inflation. Your business news app will let you know when the CPI comes out.

THE PRODUCER PRICE INDEX

To tighten up your inflation understanding and discussions, you should also watch for the Producer Price Index (PPI). This was also called the Wholesale Price Index (WPI) up to 1978 and is still sometimes referred to that way today (I think just to mess with people, but I can't prove that). The PPI looks at how much it cost a producer to make a good last year and then compares it with what it costs to make the same thing this year. This tends to give a better read on where inflation actually is than the CPI, but it is still less than perfect. It doesn't consider changes in buying patterns, and it is a measure of the prices paid by US producers and not the prices paid by consumers.

That being said, I like the PPI as a counterbalance to the CPI to gauge where inflation really is. This number is reported monthly, typically a day or two after the CPI number comes out.

THE PERSONAL CONSUMPTION EXPENDITURES INDEX

As I mentioned, there are several measures of inflation. The last one I will discuss is the price index known as Personal Consumption Expenditures (PCE). It's important because it has become the Federal Reserve's official measure of inflation.

While the Federal Reserve doesn't directly set mortgage interest rates, its actions have a huge effect on them, so we need to be aware of what it's looking at. The Fed switched to using the PCE from the CPI in 2012. The Fed did this because the PCE focuses on all expenditures as opposed to just a basket of goods. This leaves less room for things to get missed.

The PCE seems to consistently understate inflation, which may be why the Fed likes to use it. For our purposes, the PCE is a double whammy—it measures inflation and impacts interest rates. It also comes out monthly, near the end of each month. It is a little less widely known, so you may need to look it up rather than getting a push notification on your phone.

• • •

With all three of these measures in your back pocket though, you will be prepped and ready to have a strong conversation on interest rates and inflation with your customers and anyone else.

UNEMPLOYMENT RATE

Unemployment is another important indicator to watch. If people don't have jobs, they probably can't buy a home either. Like the CPI, unemployment is a relative number. When you start paying attention to it, compare the current number with the historic norms and try to get a feel for which way the economy is going.

High unemployment is typically a sign of an economy that is in a recession. A recession isn't necessarily a bad thing for real estate, as often money gets moved from things like securities, which tend to do poorly during financial downturns, to real estate. This is especially true in an inflationary market. If an economy falls into recession, one of the common things that is done to help it recover is to lower interest rates, which is beneficial to home purchasing. Unemployment is one of the easiest topics to keep on top of as it is always a major news story.

WORKFORCE PARTICIPATION RATE

Another number to watch is the workforce participation rate, which lets you know how many people are in the workforce—as opposed to the unemployment rate, which measures the number of people on unemployment. The number of people on unemployment does not reflect whether people have simply left the labor market altogether. The only way to gauge this is to look at the total number of people with jobs plus the number of people on unemployment and then compare that to what it has been in the past. This lets us know as real estate agents whether the number of potential home buyers is increasing or decreasing. If people are leaving the labor market, that means less income is being earned and fewer mortgages are being qualified for. Is there a great conversation with the customer about this topic just waiting to be had?

Could a reduction in workforce participation be an indication that the economy might not be as strong as the unemployment figures tend to indicate? If fewer people are working, that does not bode well for the strength of the economy. If the economy is weak, it will limit how aggressive the Fed will be with interest rate hikes. This means interest rates will go up less quickly than they would otherwise. This also means that the Fed will be unable to raise rates aggressively in order to curb inflation, so it may take longer to bring inflation down to normal levels. More inflation is bad for savers and bad for folks on fixed incomes, but it is very good for real estate. The workforce participation rate is not always a major headline, but the rate is always one you want to check up on to keep your conversation relevant.

GROSS DOMESTIC PRODUCT

The gross domestic product (GDP) is a measure of all the goods and services for a given country. This tells us how much stuff we sold. As you can imagine, this is pretty important when trying to stay on top of what's going on in the market in which you are asking your customers to participate.

Paying attention to GDP has paved the way for some great customer conversations. I pointed out in mid-2021 that the stock market was priced higher than it was pre-pandemic and that the GDP was lower, which meant our companies were selling less stuff but the stock prices of those companies (which are supposed to be based on their earnings) were higher than when they were selling more stuff.

When I showed customers these numbers, they all of a sudden found the idea of investing in real estate a much more interesting topic, as they felt a little less certain about the stocks they were holding. The customers who opted out of stocks and moved into real estate experienced gains of more than 20 percent, and those who stayed in the stock market experienced the pleasures of being in a bear market. The GDP is always a major headline and an easy indicator to watch out for.

THE BUILDERS CONFIDENCE INDEX

The Builders Confidence Index discloses how builders say they feel about the market. I tend to be less trusting of this number than housing starts, which I discuss next. People can say anything, but what they do with their money tends to paint a more accurate picture. That being said, this number does have value, and it is often a headline, so you need to be aware of what it is and how to discuss it.

NEW HOUSING STARTS

An important part of any market is monitoring the supply. The new housing starts measure the number of new single-family homes that started construction in a given month. This is a measure of developers putting their money where their mouth is and a tangible indication of where they think the real estate market is going.

Most developers spend a lot on research and analytics to make sure they are gauging the market properly so that they don't lose money. This can be a very good indicator of where the market is going, but not always. There are a couple of factors to keep in mind that impact housing starts: interest rates and material costs.

As we discussed earlier, interest rates have a significant impact on the economy. For builders, interest rates raise building expenses because many builders borrow the money they use to build their projects. They need to make sure the market will sustain the higher prices they will need to charge to be profitable on their projects with the additional burden of the higher interest payments they will need to make.

Similarly, higher building materials costs make homes more expensive to build, which means the home prices must increase enough to compensate for these higher materials costs. If they don't, the builder is not incentivized to build.

Longer material wait times also raise the costs to build homes. Labor is wasted when materials are not available in a timely fashion, once again making developers less motivated to start new homes.

CONSUMER CONFIDENCE

Consumer confidence measures how people feel about the economy and the future. This is important because people's spending is very much tied to this number.

When the financial outlook is poor, people tend to spend less and save more. Although our business depends on people spending their money, conservative spending is less of a problem for us than for folks selling things like jet skis, as our product meets one of the most basic human needs.

When it comes to real estate, low consumer confidence leads to uncertain buyers, and uncertain buyers make for difficult transactions. It is our job to recognize uncertainty and to give the customers what they need to feel confident with the decision they are making. Understanding when the numbers indicate that this might be more important is one reason to keep your eyes peeled for this number.

MORE CUSTOMERS FOR LIFE

This is not a comprehensive list, but if you start paying attention to these economic reports, you'll develop a better understanding of your market, the economics that drive it, and your product. That understanding will help you to provide customers with the knowledge and insights they need to make good decisions—which will enable you to build more customers for life.

All of this leads us directly into the next section: getting our customer right.

PART III

GET YOUR CUSTOMER RIGHT

CHAPTER 11

THE REAL ESTATE FIRST DATE

Communicating with Your Customers

One day my father got a call from the person that was keeping an eye on our properties in New York, and he told my father that we had a problem. One of the properties my father still owned in Red Hook in Brooklyn was a warehouse with a lot alongside it. The gentleman told my father that a weed had started to grow between the edge of the brick warehouse and the asphalt of the lot. No one had noticed the weed previously, and now it had grown to be a small tree. This happened because our family lived in Florida, so we were dependent on people to inspect the properties. My father knew if that weed did not get dealt with, it could literally bring the building down as it grew. So, he made immediate arrangements for someone to remove the weed with a chainsaw and stump grinder.

The warehouse had a tenant, Igor, who lived and worked there. When Igor saw the people my father sent to cut down the weed, he went out and basically tied himself to the weed, saying that they couldn't cut down trees like this because they beautify the neighborhood. The folks my father sent were basically of the mindset that they didn't want to deal with this BS, so they left.

My father was, to put it kindly, less than thrilled. As it turns out though, my dad and I were scheduled to go to New York about a week later, so my dad decided to deal with the weed when he got there.

We arrived and took care of all the other things we had to do in the city and then made our way over to Brooklyn. As we approached the property where Igor lived, my father stopped the car and got out. I expected to see a battle royal of my dad dressing down Igor. I figured I should have brought some milk duds or other movie candy to watch this unfold. Little did I know I was about to see a negotiation master class put on by the master himself. As I studied negotiations years later, I was able to identify the two tactics my dad used, but at the time I was just in awe of what happened.

The conversation started pleasantly enough. My dad knocked on the door, and Igor came out, and they started discussing everything in the world other than the weed. They talked about extending his lease, what the new rent would be, what was going on in local politics, etc. As my father and Igor talked, they started to move away from the front door toward the side of the building where the lot and, more importantly, where the weed was. My father looked in the lot, pointed to the weed, and said to Igor, "Can you believe that? Isn't that a shame? It's terrible when something like that is let go long enough when it can become like that. I need to get on the guys that inspect the property to not let this happen again." All of this is said as if Igor is not there.

Then my dad turned to Igor and said, "You know I sent guys to cut that thing down the other day, and somebody actually sent them away. What kind of person would do something like that?"

Igor then started to say, "Well, Bob, you know the trees make the neighborhood . . . ," at which point my father immediately interrupted, acting as if he hadn't even heard what Igor said. And now, starting to get angry, he said, "What kind of an absolute imbecile doesn't realize this could get someone really hurt? That thing will eventually bring this building down. Somebody can get killed. What kind of person has so little value for human life?"

I am editing out all the nonchurch words here, but suffice it to say that some longshoremen were blushing at this point. My dad's face was red, the vein in his forehead was out, and I was thinking to myself, "Crap, my dad is this pissed, and I am going to be stuck with him for the rest of the day."

At this point, Igor had lost all the wind in his sails and was 100 percent agreeing with my dad. He said things like, "Yes, Mr. Cadillac, the weed must go. You're right; a terrible person would be the only one to stop them from cutting it down. I think I have a knife or saw inside. Maybe I'll cut it down right now."

My dad responded, "No, Igor, and thank you, but that's not your job. I have people that will take care of that." To which Igor said, "Thank you, Mr. Cadillac."

Now, my dad and I start walking back to the car, and I think my dad is going to be upset. Instead, he turned to me and said, "You see that, son? They start with the nonsense, and you hit 'em with the one-two (to which he mimed throwing punches). Keep them off balance."

THE POST-GAME ANALYSIS

Here's why that story makes it into a chapter on how we communicate with our customers. Negotiation is a form of communication, and every customer interaction is some form of negotiation. Negotiation is the art of being persuasive. In the interaction with Igor, did my dad get exactly what he wanted? Yes, he did. Did he have to make any concessions? No, he didn't. Did Igor still like him when the negotiation was over? Yes, he did. Igor loved my dad. Good negotiation requires you to be aware of not just yourself, but the other person as well. Then you need to pick the path to achieve your goal in the best possible way with what you know of the situation.

Let's "post-game" this negotiation and see what actually happened. My dad used a mix of two tactics. First, he used a technique called "the dumb blonde" or "Columbo" method in which you act like you have less information than you do. This is very powerful for preserving relationships, as you are never accusing the other person of any wrongdoing. My dad was never mad at Igor; he was mad at the idiot who sent the people away. Igor knew who that was but could only preserve the relationship with my dad by not owning up to it.

Second, my father used another powerful technique: anger. This is where he became loud and less rational—which makes the rational arguments the other person has lined up seem ineffectual and so the person tends to abandon them. The judicious use of the right techniques achieved near perfect results.

Here's the important point: My dad was ready for the interaction before it began. That's why it was so successful So, can we do the same thing before we meet the customer for the first time?

FOCUS ON THE CUSTOMER'S HEADSPACE

Rather than focusing on ourselves and getting into the right headspace to do a listing or buyer presentation, let's focus on someone else's headspace first: the customer's. We need to convince customers to work with us, right? So, what are these experiences like from the customers' standpoint?

Let me ask you this: Have you ever been on a date where all the other person does is brag? Was that a sexy experience? Were the Barry

White or Usher greatest hits playing in your head later that evening, or were you planning another evening alone? Were you wishing you had asked your friend to make the emergency bailout call, or did you try locking eyes with the maitre d' and flashing Morse code with your eyelids to get you out of there?

As a buyer or seller of real estate, if you are interviewing an agent to potentially work with, it's kind of like that first-date experience. You're trying to decide whether you want to spend more time with this agent or if you want someone else. Unfortunately, most real estate agents act in a way that makes that first date really cringey. They come with a stack of thick matte business cards, a 368-page CMA report on the property, and a 297-page listing book that tells the history of the brokerage, their own history, letters of recommendation, and the customer's bill of rights that they printed up after a class they took that made them feel guilty they didn't have one.

Some of these folks must believe that the more trees that were cut down in the making of their presentation, the better their presentation. You might not be shocked to hear that the typical response of customers being handed these materials isn't, "Oh boy, what a page turner!" Instead, the customers wonder if they really must read all that. Or they question if they even need the agent at all, since they have to educate themselves by reading all this material anyway. Is that really the experience you want to leave the customers with? Even if you have customers that are very logical and data driven, there is a better way to introduce yourself than bringing them a small encyclopedia.

Think about the really exceptional dates you've been on—the ones where you were so engrossed in conversation that you didn't even sense time passing until the waiter tapped you on the shoulder and said, "Sorry, folks—you're going to have to leave. We're getting ready to close."

What is the difference between those dates and the train wreck dates? On the bad dates, people talk about what is interesting to *them* (which is themselves, their company, and their standards). On the good ones, they're talking about something that's interesting to *both* parties. So, what I say to agents is, "Your customers are interested in entering the real estate market, and they have brought in a real estate market expert. What do you think they might want to talk about before engaging with the real estate market?" (Said another way, what can you almost guarantee that they will be interested in talking about with a real estate market expert?)" If you guessed the real estate market, you are absolutely correct."

GETTING READY FOR THE FIRST DATE

The conversation topic is pretty basic: the market, how supply and demand are affecting it, and what the customer wants to do. So, you need to be prepared to have a high-quality conversation about what is going on in the market and why; whether it's a good or bad thing for the customer; and what the implications are going forward. If you do this well, I can almost guarantee that you'll have a fascinated customer on your hands. The importance of having this type of informed conversation can't be overstated. If done properly, it handles many of the big issues agents tend to have with customers.

What you want to communicate to your customers is that your entire presentation is about helping them achieve their goals and that you have the skills to do that for them. In order to have the interaction go well, you need to deal with a few things first. You want to be well prepared. Rather than printing those giant reports, you should spend your time boning up on the market where the property is. We will talk about more specifics on this later in the book.

Next, you need to be in the right headspace when you go into this meeting. Your mental approach will affect how the customer responds and your ability to deal with any rejections you have along the way. Yes, rejection happens. It is a part of the business. I don't want to be surprised when it rears its ugly head. I need to have a game plan that allows me to deal with it and learn from it.

Dealing with rejection is important in our business, because if we don't, we can easily become demotivated, miserable, and even depressed. Are any of those conducive to closing business? The answer is a resounding no.

Earlier, I discussed managing your mental state. You need to be in the right place to be compelling and attractive to your customer. That means if you have just finished three hours of cold calling, do not go directly into a listing meeting. Why? Because cold calls have one of the highest rates of rejection of any activity in our industry. The rejection from the cold calls will manifest itself in your presentation. Before you leave, you need to invest in getting yourself back to feeling like a winner.

For starters, you are not weird or a loser. One thing that may help you is knowing that everyone feels that way occasionally, and getting rejected and feeling down is a normal part of this business. If you feel like nothing is ever going to work out, think all you do is lose, and start wondering why you even got out of bed today, it doesn't mean anything is wrong with you. The most successful people in the industry have felt that way at times. Do you wish they told you that when you started in the business, huh? I tell agents that "if you haven't cried yourself to sleep at least once in this business, then you are probably doing something wrong." So, being down is normal. Staying down is a choice. You need to answer the question, what are you going to do about it?

We can't stay down, because it is super unattractive to our customers, and it makes us less good at the job they are depending on us to do for them. We need to have an emergency plan to get ourselves back up when we are down. This is where the CEO in you needs to step up and to know what motivates the staff to keep them on track.

This can be as simple as listening to a song that gets your juices flowing again or watching a video on YouTube that makes you feel driven to never give up. You want to enact your emergency mood plan when you as the CEO sense the morale of the staff is not good and you need to perform in front of customers soon. You are your own HR department, so it's up to you to keep yourself motivated to succeed and to have a great attitude for your "first date."

WATCH YOUR BODY LANGUAGE

Your body language is a huge hinderance or opportunity in your interaction with customers. It affects how you are perceived and how much weight people give to what you say. What your body portrays typically reflects your mental state, which is why we talked about your mind first.

We need to be aware of what our body is saying when we aren't saying anything. Body language that is calm and confident will go a long way to attracting people to you. When we discuss rapport, we will talk more about good body language, but for now I want to help you to avoid the biggest trap agents fall into that pushes customers away: coming off as desperate.

Have you ever been on a date with someone who came off as desperate? Let me ask you, was it sexy or not sexy? The answer—not very sexy at all. Being desperate will make even otherwise attractive people seem less so, because their body language naturally makes us feel like there is a reason why they are desperate. That makes them seem less attractive and therefore less desirable to date or work with.

One of the best ways to not seem desperate is to reduce the consequences of the interaction in your own mind. If I am thinking, "Oh my God, if I don't get this listing I am going to starve," odds are my body language is going to be way too needy. But suppose I am thinking something more like, "This is a chance to work on my listing presentation for when I'm doing one for real. Let's see how this one goes, and I can tighten my conversation skills as a bonus. One way or the other, I am treating myself to an ice cream cone when I'm done."

Now for anyone that knows me, you know that the promise of ice cream will have me in a great mood the whole time I am speaking. If you don't like ice cream (not sure we could be friends), then perhaps tofu and kale are what make you happy and give you something to look forward to. The reason to do this is that excitement and desperation create pretty similar body language cues. I want to have something that makes me excited because that energy will come through in my presentation as excitement and help any desperation that might sneak through to just be perceived by my customer as more excitement. For agents that are trying to learn how to get better results with customers, this is a very useful trick. That little thing I give myself to look forward to is strictly a tool to help me manage my mental state. I am not rewarding failure by promising this in advance to myself. I am allowing myself to think that regardless of what happens, there is a happy outcome waiting for me. This will help reduce the pressure I feel while actually doing the thing at which I want to succeed.

THE BIG THREE

Remember that the goal of this entire interaction is to close a customer for life, and that means we don't want to seem like the stereotypical real estate agent that most customers expect. Instead, we want to be what they actually really need—a well-informed professional that will help them to achieve their goals. This requires us to give them three things to meet their desires and in the process to close customers for life—and they are:

1. Rapport
2. Credibility
3. Trust

I call these the big three. If what we are saying or doing in the inter-action is not adding to one of those three categories, it needs to go. Everything we say in our presentation needs to have a purpose. We do need to ask customers questions to understand their particular circumstances, but that shouldn't be what drives this interaction. We are the expert in the room, so we need to drive things.

Talking to customers can be a lot like playing tennis. If I were going to play tennis with Rafael Nadal, I would immediately need to rebrand what a good day on a tennis court looks like. As a person that has never really played tennis before, I would probably consider me getting to anything he hit and making contact with my racket to be a win. That is how most agents handle the interactions with their customers, especially when it comes to objections. Their customers hit the ball to them, and the agents are just hoping to survive. The problem with that is we are not the amateur in the interaction; we are the professional. What do you think Nadal is trying to do with every single ball he hits? He is trying to score. As the professional, we need to score points on everything we say. What are points, you ask? Points are anything that builds the big three. Building your game as a professional means eliminating things that don't score points.

The last thing to discuss here is emotional transference. Your emotional state is felt by your customer. Have you ever been on a date with someone who was tense? Everything may have gone perfectly but the person was nervous. How did you feel? Uncomfortable, tense, nervous? Was that a positive experience? What makes you think it would be a pleasant one for our customer if we came across as tense.

On the other hand, have you ever been on a date where things didn't go perfectly, but the other person was super relaxed about it and laughing? How did you feel? It was more pleasant than the other date, wasn't it? If your answer is no, you may be the tense one from the previous example. For most people, the person that is more relaxed and having a good time is much more pleasant to be around and is thus far more attractive.

This chapter seems like it could be from a dating advice book in some places. The reason for that is simple: The correlation between dating and auditioning to enter into a relationship with a customer is hard to overstate. Yes, there is a far less chance of making out in the back seat of your car with a real estate interaction, but there is a far greater chance of building a lifelong relationship that will support your business for years to come. So, in summary, tighten up your customer "dating" game to start closing customers for life.

CHAPTER 12

KNOWING HOW TO BUILD AND USE RAPPORT

When I was a kid, my father wanted to make sure he taught my brother and me responsibility. We had just moved to a property that had 2½ acres of land, and for my father, who was a lifelong city dweller, this constituted a lot of land. He decided we should have a small farm and petting zoo on the property. Cue to the *Green Acres* theme song. My father was driven to do things for kids that didn't have much. He thought it would be nice for the kids at the school where we ran the cafeteria operation to visit our place for field trips. In addition, the farm would provide the aforementioned responsibility lesson for his two boys. What could go wrong?

All we needed were the animals, so we found a farmer who was leaving the country and was selling all his farm animals. My brother and I were maybe six and eight years old, respectively (yeah, my dad believed in starting work young), and so the trip to this farm was an amazing adventure. We were going to take animals home! What could be better? Ah, the ignorance of youth!

At the farm, there were ducks, geese, swans, chickens, and lots of other animals. My father wasn't too naïve, so he knew better than to get a horse, but he did buy quite a few animals, including a bunch of peacocks. The whole time we were walking around the farm, my father and the farmer were chatting, and they really seemed to hit it off.

As we were getting ready to leave, my brother and I were totally fixated on a yellow Labrador retriever named Sasha. My parents had pug dogs when I grew up. They were cute and snored like Sherman tanks without a muffler, but that was pretty much all they did. Now, here was a dog that you throw a ball to, and she gets it and brings it back to you. In fact, if you threw it near her, she would even catch it—often displaying incredible athleticism in the process. My brother and I were awestruck. We had no idea these feats of canine athleticism existed in the real world. Being eight and six, we possessed the child-like superpower of persuasion, so we both turned the doe-eyed look on our dad with the requisite, "Daddy, can we please get the dog too?"

As it turned out, the dog sufficiently impressed my dad too, so he asked the farmer if he would sell the dog. He hemmed and hawed, and finally said, "It is a family dog, and my kids love her. I don't think it would be right." He also said when they moved, they planned to take the dog with them.

The farmer did come up with an idea though. He told my dad if he took the donkey and the llama, he would throw in the dog. He wanted $400 for the donkey and $1,000 for the llama. My father and the farmer had built some rapport and were getting along really well, and so my dad said, "Hey look, I'm not a farmer, and we are just trying to get a few animals for the kids to take care of. We aren't ready to have both animals. Will you cut me a break, and if I take the donkey, will you throw in the dog?" The farmer thought about it and said he would.

THE DONKEY AND THE LLAMA

This deal got done because the farmer and my dad developed a rapport, and it continued because my dad felt like he got a good deal. That was until the first night after the donkey arrived.

The donkey was young and not used to being alone. He cried all night. We could hear it in the house, and as tough minded as my dad was, he could never stand to see an animal in pain. He called the farmer and told him about the situation. The farmer said, "I was worried about that. The donkey was recently weened, and that can happen. He is crying because he is lonely."

My dad asked how long this typically would go on for, and the farmer said it could be a while. My dad asked if there was a solution, and the farmer said, "Well the donkey did have a friend he grew up with that if he was there, it would probably cure the loneliness and he would stop crying."

My dad said, "OK, as long as it stops the poor donkey from crying. It's breaking my heart."

So that's how I grew up with a donkey and a llama, and why we never went to a farm again. Sometimes even a master negotiator like my dad doesn't get the best end of a deal.

I realized that the rapport my father and the farmer built was a powerful tool they both used to get the deal done. The farmer used his knowledge and the natural curiosity of my dad to engage in conversation that my father found interesting and allowed the relationship to build. Because of the rapport building the farmer did, my father considered what it would be like to move to a new country and try to get rid of a bunch of animals.

THE IMPORTANCE
AND LIMITS OF RAPPORT

People like doing deals with people they like and often will take less favorable terms to preserve that relationship. Rapport helps to humanize you in other people's eyes and makes them consider how their decisions will affect your life. They start to, in some small way, care about you and your life. This has a softening position on the totally logical arguments they have and allows emotion to work its way in to weaken their negotiating position. Rapport can be an effective tool to make people happy at the prospect of making you happy by working with you, and it can be an effective tie breaker when a customer has to decide between you and another agent.

This is where rapport's power needs to end in your calculation though. Our industry is tripping all over itself with techniques and tactics to try to build rapport. Brokers, agents, and instructors behave like rapport is the end-all and be-all to earn a customer's business. I have a problem with this. Sure, rapport is powerful, but it completely misses the reason the customer sought out an agent to begin with. Do you suppose that the customer was sitting at home watching Netflix with a big bowl of popcorn, thinking, "I'm really lonely. You know what I need to fix that right up? I need a real estate agent." Is that the customer's thought process? Are customers coming to us because they lack friends? The answer is no. The one thing real estate customers always have when they work with an agent is a real estate problem that they do not feel equipped to solve themselves.

If their real estate problem is what drives them to seek us out, then maybe instead of leading off with making the case for what a great friend we could be, we should start by showing them how well equipped we are to solve their real estate problems. Novel idea, huh? Figure out what the customers need and then give it to them. Guess what? When you give them what they need, it builds rapport too. This is a matter of putting the horse in front of the cart. I am not going to go into the relationship trying to make a friend that gives me business due to our friendship. I am going in to show that I can solve the person's problem and that I can do it better than anyone else, and in the process, we will become friends for life.

Rapport by itself is not enough. Have you ever had great rapport with a customer (I mean, you guys are clicking like crazy), only for that customer to turn around and use another agent? If you haven't, then you must be new to the industry, as this happens to all agents at some point. Maybe asking this question a different way would make it clearer. Do you have a friend who if the person walked in the room right now, you would get a huge smile on your face? The kind of friend that tells the best and funniest stories. You know the one I mean. The one that's a little wild and crazy.

The friend I'm talking about is the one that tells the story of going to the concert, sneaking backstage, and winding up being invited to a party with the rock band. He tells how he was in the back of the limo, and someone offered him something out of a little plastic baggy to try. He tells you he still doesn't know what it was, but after he took some, he decided the thing he wanted to do was strip off all his clothes and run naked through the woods. Unfortunately, a bear inhabited that forest, and your friend assures you that the affinity of bears for honey is not overstated. So, this tale of pharmaceutical experimentation rapidly devolves into a chase, with the bear chasing and your friend desperately running away. Just before the bear is about to get him, your friend manages to jump over someone's fence and escape.

This story once again reminds you how amazed you are that your friend does not have a police record. Here is the question though: Is this friend the first person you call when you need a babysitter? The answer for anything approaching a responsible parent is "Hell no!" But you have such great rapport with this friend. Your friend makes you smile, makes you laugh. It is still not enough!

As agents, rapport does not get us where we need to be. It can help, but you can't buy into the mainstream real estate garbage that asserts rapport is more important than anything else. Actions like answering questions with questions, mirroring body language, and keeping the customer talking are all examples of rapport building at the expense of establishing yourself as the person who can solve the customer's problems. That is my warning of taking rapport too far. That being said, it is still a powerful tool when used well, so let's look at how to do that.

FOCUS ON THE CUSTOMERS

Whenever you start to work with prospective customers, the first most critical thing you need to focus on is gathering data. You need to know what matters to them and what their motivations are. *Why* are they looking to buy or sell a property, what things concern them, what benefits do they think they will achieve, and if they found me, why do they want the type of property they came to me with interest in? That data is going to allow me to direct my conversation in a way that will be most helpful and interesting to the potential customers. People like folks that are helpful and interesting, and so the rapport building begins.

For example, let's say a customer comes in and tells me she wants to talk about doing a real estate deal with crypto. One option would be to use a regular, cookie-cutter–type approach and just treat her like a standard customer. But just by telling me that she's a crypto investor, I know that she has done one of the hardest things we do as Americans: forgone instant gratification by putting her hard-earned money into an investment. This gives me a tremendous amount of insight into how I need to talk to her in order to build rapport. I can tailor my remarks to her investment interest and show that I'm on the same page. Unless there's some other personality clash, that customer is almost guaranteed to end up liking me because I'm speaking exactly to her concerns.

This is especially important during listing conversations with a seller. Real estate is a competitive industry, and listing meetings are generally where I meet the sellers for the first time and try to convince them to let me be the one to sell their home. At the end of these conversations, my personal goal is for the sellers to have no more than one or two very specific or unusual questions for me. I want to use my presentation to preemptively answer everything they intended to ask, proving that I've thought about them in advance, paid attention, and understand what matters to them. If I can do this, chances are high that I'll get the listing.

Rapport shows that you are the kind of person they want to be around. It says, "Hey, I am fun to be with." This is great because it will give you a leg up in getting them to agree to work with you. It is an important part of the big three things (rapport, credibility, and trust) we need to close customers for life. So, let's talk about some simple and practical things you can do to increase your rapport building.

RAPPORT-BUILDING TECHNIQUES

One thing that you can completely control and has a profound effect on people is the energy level you bring to the interaction. If you come in with lower energy than the folks you are trying to talk to, they will feel it as a drain. If you come in at their level, they feel nothing, and thus you receive no benefit from it. If you come in with a much higher energy level than theirs, they start to wonder just how much Red Bull you had right before talking to them. The area you want to shoot for is energy that is a bit higher than that of your listeners. This will bring everyone's energy level up, and that will be felt as a positive in your favor.

People are attracted to people with good energy levels. When I teach a class, I am very cognizant of my energy level. I know as a student it makes all the difference in the world. If the instructor has good energy, I will enjoy the class and will learn more. You are going to be doing a lot of teaching to your customers in your role as real estate market expert, so make their learning a joy by being energetic and excited with your approach.

It seems so simple, but a smile makes an amazing difference in how people perceive you. The value of this is often underrated by those who have not seen the power this wields. I remember reading a book on the power of a smile and thinking to myself this is BS. It can't make that much of a difference. I decided to try it though. At that time, I was training and dieting to get into competition shape as a body builder. I was running my Italian restaurants back then, and there was not anything there that I could eat. Instead, each night after we closed the restaurant, I drove to a local TGI Fridays and ordered a New York strip and some broccoli. I would do this pretty much five nights a week. I was a regular, to say the least.

Everyone knew me who worked there. The hostesses would just say, "Hey, Josh, just you? I'd say "Yep," and they'd give me a table. The server would come over and ask if I wanted the usual. The staff would be pleasant, and we might chat for a couple of minutes about how I was doing or what book I was reading, but that would be it. This is where I decided to implement the plan. I started smiling intentionally when I talked to everyone. Within the course of a couple of weeks, my table would be surrounded by people that worked there. Not just the hostesses or my server, but all the servers from the whole place would come by and talk to me.

It got to the point that the manager would come out and make everyone get back to work. Then the manager would sit and talk to me as I ate my dinner 'cause the silly smile worked on him too.

Too few people smile in this world. Look at the miserable faces around you and decide to be something different. It is a gift you can give to everyone you speak to, and it costs you nothing. Truth be told, it makes you feel better too.

Some agents think that they must be super serious when talking to customers, and any crack in their ice-cold stoic facade will destroy their chance of being taken seriously. Nothing could be further from the truth. You should never be afraid to be funny. Laughter can be great medicine, much like the smile above. If you can tell a story that gets people laughing, maybe even one that pokes fun at yourself a little bit, it can do a lot to show that you don't take yourself too seriously. This can be a great counterbalance to some of the things you might need to say to build your credibility, which we will discuss in the next chapter. If you can let people know you are a rock star at what you do but aren't afraid to poke fun at yourself, it is an amazing sweet spot for customers. They want someone good, but they don't want to work with an arrogant jerk.

GETTING INTO A TALKATIVE STATE

Controlling how you feel on the way into an interaction with a customer is another great way to build rapport. As mentioned before, if you are nervous, your customers will feel that and be nervous and tense; and if you are comfortable, they will feel comfortable. If you've ever been on a date with someone who is very tense and nervous, you know it doesn't make you feel good.

It is common to say, "I need to be more confident," but for most people that is a very nebulous statement and really hard to figure out how to implement. Here's a tip: Not making the interaction about you and instead focusing on making the customer comfortable is a great tool to achieve being perceived as more confident. For many people, it is actually easier to try to relax so they don't make someone else nervous than it is for them to will themselves to be less nervous. To create a comfortable atmosphere in your presentations, don't make your presentations about you; make them about the customers' comfort instead.

Getting yourself ready to be personable is an important part of being prepared for customer interactions that build rapport. Parts of the job of being a real estate agent involve working quietly for long periods of time and not speaking to anyone. For most people, going from dead silence to a high-energy, good mood ready for a fun and fluid conversation is not a light switch that's easy to flip. You want to warm up in order to be in a talkative state. This is the mental equivalent of stretching before engaging in an athletic activity.

Especially if you are going to be doing something like cold calling, you need to focus on reaching that talkative state. This is when your mind is really working well, when you can make jokes about the things people say and get them to laugh, and you can exude good humor in general. This is the state where you can be a little over the top. Saying something at the start of a phone call like "You know I had a note to call someone awesome today, and well, now you know why I called you" is something that people don't hear often, and it makes their day a little better. That line is only appropriate for some conversations, but it is a way to avoid sounding like a salesperson, and at the same time it brings joy and value to the customer. Plus, it tends to put the listeners in a better mood and helps boost them to a talkative state. The "yeses" we need in our business from customers are much more likely to occur when we get our customers to join us in that talkative state.

One of the other secret powers of rapport building is that if you are good at it, you can get people to tell you things they otherwise wouldn't. This is a skill I am still working on, but I do know someone that is the ultimate tenth-degree black belt in this conversational martial art. Guessing you are expecting another story about my dad, but no. The ultimate champion of this is my mom. I am convinced that if the Russians had her interrogating our captured spies, America would have lost the cold war. I have watched this from a distance with sheer mystification.

My mom is this super-sweet, kind, and genuine lady from the Midwest. The people she does this to never see it coming and don't even realize it's happening. She simply has a conversation with them, and they then divulge things that they have never told anyone in their life. I have had several people tell me, "Hey, man, I was just talking to your mom." At this point they have a look of bewilderment and are shaking their head and then say something like, "I have to watch what I say around your mom. She just asks me questions, and she's so interested I wind up watching the words come out of my mouth and can't take them back, and I sit there and wonder how she got me to say that." At the same time, every one of these folks loves my mom.

This kind of rapport building is the next level. It gets people to confide in you. This is important to help facilitate the type of rapport we want to help close customers for life. Giving people the sense that they can tell you the truth reflects good relationship building. The way this is done is by being genuinely interested in people and getting them talking. (Now, I need to place the caveat that this is a secondary goal. When it comes to the real estate conversations, you need to be doing most of the talking.)

My mom has told me that she doesn't think about what she is going to say; she just simply asks the next question to find out more about the (very interesting) person she is talking to. Here is the secret: Everyone wants to be interesting, and to my mom everyone is. The experience of having someone who is not flattering you, but is genuinely being fully engaged and present for what you are saying, is a thing most people seldom if ever get to enjoy.

The time and place for these types of conversations is after your credibility has been established. When you are in the process of finding out more about potential customers, you should pursue this type of rapport building. Remember, however, that your first job is to prove to them that you can do the thing that made them come to you in the first place: You can solve their real estate problems.

In the process of convincing them you can solve their real estate problems, you build rapport, earn their confidence, and eventually learn their secrets. This allows you to serve the customers in the best way possible. The important thing to remember is that you don't want to know things they might not want to tell you in order to hurt them. You want them to feel comfortable telling you those types of things because it will allow you to better understand them and to better meet their needs. When you've achieved that kind of relationship, it indicates that you are well on your way to closing a customer for life.

CHAPTER 13

USING KNOWLEDGE TO BUILD CREDIBILITY

After working with my dad for a few years and when I had reached the ripe old age of 13, he decided it was time for me to get some management experience. He had a couple of guys that were more than 10 years my senior start working with me. I was supposed to be their boss. My dad would give me the orders for what he wanted done, and it was my job to get my crew to make it happen.

As you can imagine, taking orders from a little kid wasn't super well received by the two guys, and there were some growing pains I had to go through. My dad told me that if I wanted my crew to respect me, I needed to be above reproach. This meant I needed to be there before they got there, work as hard as or harder than any of them, and always know what I was talking about. The first two things he said are all about setting an example, but the last one was all about being prepared.

My dad said, "If you get to a jobsite and then start to think about what you will need and what you are going to do, you are a fool. No crew wants to work with a fool. If your people know (or think they know) more than you, it will be a problem."

His solution for this was to start every job by first developing what he called "a bill of materials." This meant I needed to think through every single thing I would need to get the job done. If my job stopped because I forgot to buy one special screw, that 50 cent screw would end up costing far more than the 50 cents because of lost labor time while someone goes to Home Depot to get the screw. In addition, we lose credibility because we look like we don't know what the heck we're doing.

When it comes to real estate, we don't have to do a lot of example setting for our customers (with a few exceptions), but we do need to develop their respect. The previous chapter was all about using your personality to get people to like you and want to work with you. This chapter is about showing that you know so much that they can't imagine doing the deal without you on their team.

I often ask in classes what is the first and most important negotiation you have with the customer. I provide a hint by telling the members of the class that this negotiation can begin before they ever meet the customer. Agents will guess things like how we determine the commission, how we show the property, how we get preapproved, etc. None of these are correct, and because agents don't recognize this first negotiation, they don't realize what they need to do to win it. The correct answer is the first case you need to make in any real estate transaction with a new customer is that you know what the hell you are talking about.

The seller and agent are in a showdown about who is the true real estate expert in the room. Many customers think we are lazy, not very smart, and overpaid when we meet them, because that's what they think of real estate agents in general. It is up to you on the way in the door to let them know that the opinion they have of other agents might be true of them, but it's wrong in regard to you. If your customers begin a sentence with, "Yeah, but I saw on Zillow . . . ," it is a clear indicator that you have not won the credibility negotiation. They've alerted you that they think that they, with the benefit of a website, know more than you and are therefore the true real estate market expert in the room. It's just like how doctors must feel when patients reference something they read on WebMD. So glad they went to medical school too, right?

If you allow your customers to know more about your product than you, then don't be surprised if they start to think of you as super-fluous. Their asking you to cut your commission is an example of how this manifests itself. In general, requests for you to reduce your compensation are a clear indication that the customers don't feel that you bring sufficient value to the table with what you do and shows you haven't established much credibility. If they value you, they will pay you.

If you are getting hit with commission cut requests, it's a clear indication that you are failing to prenegotiate. You have a choice. You can wait for the customer to ask for a commission cut, or you can start establishing so much credibility as you walk in the door that the customer would never even think of asking you to cut your commission. That might sound impossible, but I have only been asked twice in the past 10 years to cut my commission. Both times I was asked to do it were because the customer had been referred to me and started the conversation off with, "Hey, Josh, so-and-so told me you are the only guy to talk to about this real estate thing I want to do. What do you charge"? There is no way to stop that one, because there is no opportunity before that to negotiate for credibility and establish what you bring to the table.

Credibility cuts off a ton of problems before they begin. Think about this: How often do people go to the chief of surgery for a procedure they need and question how the surgeon intends to hold the scalpel, suggest a different company's surgical products, or ask for a discount? Do you want to cut that type of crap out? Establish that you are a person deserving of respect by winning the negotiation for credibility.

How do we do that though? It ties back to the story at the start of this chapter. We need a bill of materials that consists of answers and proof that we know what we need in order to own the type of transaction the customers are looking to do. This means we need to think about the people who are often forgotten, our customers. Not thinking about them as adversaries (that we do in real estate way too much), but as what they are, people with a real estate problem they don't trust themselves to solve on their own.

The reason our customers find us is because they are scared that they don't know how to solve their real estate problem. All the studies bear this out. If you look at the reasons customers give when asked why they chose to use an agent, their reasons are all fear-based. The customers may cite being intimidated by the contract, finding the right house, and negotiating the price, along with a bunch of other things, but every one of those is based in a fear that without a professional to guide them, they will make a mistake.

The way to be successful in a capitalist society is to consider what the customers need and figure out how to get it to them better than they can get it someplace else. If they are scared, then you need to establish that if they have you, they don't need to be afraid because you really know how to solve real estate problems. This would speak directly to their fear and show them that you are thinking about what it's like to be them. What type of person do you want to be around when you are scared? What would be most meaningful and helpful to allay your fears?

Most agents never consider this about their customers. They don't recognize the fear that the customers bring with them. They think because the customers cite Zillow, their favorite real estate YouTube channel, or HGTV, that the customers are being impossible and stubborn. The reality is, most customers think very little of real estate agents, and they educate themselves to protect themselves from us.

In my customer's mind I don't start off on an equal footing with the customer. I am starting off at the bottom of a well, and I need to dig my way out to be taken seriously as a professional. Here is the big secret: Customers are desperate to find an agent who proves their low opinion of all agents is wrong. The customers are dying to find an agent they respect.

Because I understand this, I try to establish my credibility early. I want to put my customers at ease as soon as possible. I want them to feel like they are hiring the 800-pound gorilla in the room. For most people, if they are standing by the bar and start to turn around and someone who is not paying attention carelessly runs into them, they might be initially irate. If they turn and see that the person they collided with is almost seven feet tall and a shade over 350 pounds with "born to kill" tattooed across the forehead, most folks will immediately say something like, "Excuse me, sir. I really need to watch more carefully where I'm going." Why? Because they are scared. If in the same situation, they have their fiercely loyal 800-pound gorilla named Bubbah with them, they probably say something more like, "Hey! Watch where you're walking. Are we gonna have a problem here? Bubbah, get 'em!" They're not scared because they have confidence in the strength of the person they are with. I want my customers to almost feel sorry for the other side when they turn me loose on them. Why? Because when I'm scared, that's what I want someone to make me feel like.

If you were on trial for murder, whom would you want representing you? Somebody kind, with a winning smile, nice eyes, and a business card that features the person with their dog and kids? Or would you want the attorney that needs to be tested for rabies, that knows every trick in the book, and that other attorneys fear? Would it be someone who would get up there and fight aggressively and effectively on your behalf? Folks, when the stakes are as high as they are in a murder case or in the largest financial transaction most people ever do (real estate), people will pick "good" over "nice" almost every time. Luckily for us we don't have to choose. We can be both. This is the fundamental reason rapport is insufficient. It misses the customer's mental state.

THINGS TO FEAR

This also means that our customer's fear is actually what provides our job security. Is the list of things the customer knows to be scared of in real estate comprehensive? If you look at the things customers are afraid of, some of the biggest ones that should be on the list aren't included. This is because the customers don't do this for a living. I want the customers to know everything they need to be afraid of. They need to know everything I plan to do to protect them so they can see the value of what I bring to the table. Things like:

- Lowball offers
- No-call, no-show showing appointments
- Home inspections
- Bad appraisals
- Bad contractors
- Title issues and slow lenders
- The lending process
- Lack of communication from the other side

These things never make the customer's list of things to be concerned about; yet most agents know they can and often do cause huge issues that can cost the customer. I imagine agents don't want to tell customers about these things because they feel like they will talk them out of the deal or perhaps out of working with them.

Since I know fear is what brought my customers to me, I am going to tell them about everything else they need to be afraid of too. I then tell them what I am going to do to mitigate all the risks on the list and how I will handle them so they will not be an issue. That helps keep my customers with me. Let's look at a few from that list.

Lowball Offers

An example I use all the time is lowball offers. When you get any offer in, you are required to send it to your customer in a timely manner, according to our code of ethics. So, when you get a lowball offer, that means you must send it to the seller. Correct? But how does your customer feel when receiving that super-low offer? Most of the time the customer is angry, and the crazy thing is, the customer is often mad at you.

I guess the customer thinks that you called the other agent up and said, "Hey, you know what would really make my day? If you could send me a ridiculously low offer, that I know will piss off my customer and has absolutely no chance of succeeding that I am ethically required to send to the customer; that would be amazing." As agents, we hate lowball offers too, because we know our customers get mad.

This happens frequently. Agents know this and do nothing about it. Why? Because they are too busy lead sourcing and monitoring their social media to give a crap about something as trivial as this. The problem is, it potentially sours their customer's experience of working together with them. Let's fix this. Something you need to understand is you have one of two options you can choose when it comes to problems:

1. You could be the prophet that prognosticated what could happen in the future, told the customer what you would do if it did happen, and then did it.

2. You could be seen in the customer's eyes as the idiot who didn't know it could happen and is now playing damage control to try and preserve your commission.

That's it, folks, only two options. Option two is not conducive to closing customers for life, and option one requires you to think and plan ahead. You will need to do your homework on Friday night after school instead of waiting till the bus ride to school on Monday morning if you want to build a business.

So how do we fix the lowball-offer issue? We get out in front of it. During the listing presentation, you want to discuss with your customer the way the offer and counteroffer process works. You want to tell your seller that no matter how perfectly we price the property, offers will come in that often will be far less than the amazing price that we have the property on the market for. You need to explain that they—as the sellers—have the control with any offer that comes in. They could say yes, no, or "Not at that price, but we will at this price." This is where I handle the lowball. I tell the sellers, "If an offer comes in that is way too low and it makes you upset, you can let me do my favorite thing." "

They typically ask me, "What is that?"

I tell them, "I will counter by quoting the buyers a higher price than the original asking price." The house is listed for $400,000; the offer comes in for $238,000, I counter at $1,134,549 and blind-copy my customer on the email. When the agent calls up spluttering and spitting, demanding to know where my counter came from, I respond that it came from the same place their offer did.

Here's the question: How do my customers feel when I do that for them? Do you think they feel protected? Looked out for? That as their agent, I knew what could happen and told them what I'd do about it and then did it? This is an easy fix. Lowball offers is a thing that happens to agents all the time and by not coming up with a solution they have allowed to adversely affect their customer's experience of the transaction. Why wouldn't we have a solution for this? The answer is, there is no excuse. Not having a solution means we failed to think of how this affects our customer because we had not prepared a "bill of materials" of the answers we would need to provide.

No-Call, No-Show Showing Appointments

In our industry, it is so common for agents to make appointments to show properties and not call to cancel if they're not going to be there and not show up, it is an epidemic. Everyone in the industry knows it, but we do nothing to prepare our customers for it. When this happens to my customers, and they wait for an agent who doesn't show, they get mad at me. Let's fix it. Once again, we need to get out in front of this. During the listing presentation we need to let the seller know that this is something that could happen and that it is entirely outside of our control to stop. I tell them, "What I need for you to do to help mitigate this is, anytime an agent schedules with you to see your home, write down the agent's name and the company the agent is with. If the agent doesn't show up, you let me know. I will send an email to the agent's broker to let the broker know exactly what happened and how ridiculously unprofessional this is."

That email will address how not showing a basic courtesy like this is entirely unacceptable, and I hope that it is not indicative of how people do things at the brokerage or how the brokers train their agents. Behavior like this is the very reason agents and our industry are held in such low esteem. This message goes on from there. It is a saved email template. If my customer gets no call and is no-showed, I simply copy the template, insert the agent's name, look up the broker, add the broker's name as well, and send the email to the broker. Of course, I do that while blind-copying my customer on the email. It's not enough to do it. The customer needs to see you doing it. Once again, how do my customers feel when they see that I am more upset about this than they are?

Home Inspections

These pose a lot of risk to the seller if issues they had no idea about are discovered that they must now fix and/or disclose going forward. This can be very nerve-racking for sellers. There are a couple of ways to deal with this. First off, let them know how it works. Tell them that they could have an agreed-upon price and still be in a place where the deal gets canceled, or they have to give a credit. One thing to keep in mind when working with sellers is, they lose all negotiating power in the real estate transaction as soon as they sign their contract. There is really only one direction prices go after that point—down.

There are two major potential bites that the buyer gets at the seller's apple: home inspection and the appraisal. Do you think 800-pound gorillas like people biting their customers' apples? If not, then we shouldn't either. So, option one: Have the sellers pay for their own home inspection. This allows them to be made aware of any issues and gives them a chance to predisclose them or make repairs. The predisclosure part is important because so many contracts are of the as-is variety in the industry today, but even if not, this still works in your favor.

If you receive your seller's permission and disclose the seller-paid home inspection as an attachment in your MLS, along with any receipts for repairs, then all offers that come in should have taken this information into account. When someone submits an offer on your customer's property, it is supposed to be based on all known information about the condition of the property. You've made a very thorough disclosure. Many times buyers will opt to save the money and not get their own home inspection report if the seller has already paid for a report and has disclosed it. If the buyers do opt to pay for their own report and then try to bring up something already dis-closed, you can claim their offer was made in bad faith. While that claim is true and what they are doing is not ethical, it is not some-thing that you can use to get someone in trouble typically. What the claim of negotiating in bad faith does do is pull a lot of the wind out of the buyers' sails when looking to negotiate for a credit, and it puts your customer in the position of being in the right. That can help a lot, as negotiation is persuasion.

The other option is to let your sellers know that if the buyer has requested repairs, the costs of the repairs quoted by the buyer or their home inspector are typically too high and a starting place for negotiation. We will get real estimates to get the things repaired (not replaced if possible). If appropriate, we will tell the sellers that we will remind the buyer's agent this was not a new home, something the buyer knew. It is not reasonable to expect brand-new things to replace older things. One other tool you can tell the seller we can use to bridge the gap would be a home warranty. This would mitigate the reasonable risk the buyer would have of something that was repaired breaking and needing to be replaced.

Bad Appraisals

This is the other thing that often gives the buyer a bite at my sellers' apple. When discussing this with the sellers, let them know that many agents don't understand the process, which can be an issue to overcome. For those that do know the appraiser's job, there are ways to help get the appraiser to bring the value in where it should be. Conventional real estate knowledge says the agent should meet the appraiser at the property with coffee, doughnuts, and three active and three closed comps that are the best comps and also support the contract price.

The three active and three closed comps come from the fact that this is what is typically shown in the appraisal form. Agents don't realize that the appraiser has to look at all the comps to find the best ones, not just the ones that support the price. What you need to do is bring the three active and three closed comps you like, as well as all the other comps that might be relevant with your notes on them about why they are not as good as the comps you used. This helps the appraisers to make the case on their report and to respond if they are questioned about why they used the comps they did. It also has the added benefit of showing them that you know how a valuation is done, which means if the appraisal doesn't come in with a reasonable valuation, you are the type of agent that will be a pain in their butt.

Appraisers don't like it when their values are challenged. If they think you will do it and do it persuasively, they are much more likely to try to avoid a situation that makes you want to challenge the appraisal. One other tip would be, if you are in a multiple-offer situation with multiple high offers, then show these other offers to the appraiser to show that there are multiple people willing to pay a similar amount for the property.

Title Issues and Slow Lenders

This is a bit of a two-for-one. Most title issues can be fixed with time. For this reason, I often request the buyer to send me a contract with a shorter closing date and an extension rather than a contract for the full date. I do this because both the title company and the lender prioritize files based on how much time they have to close those files. If the buyer's mortgage broker has been bragging about being able to close FHA deals in 21 days and the agent sends me an offer with 45 days on it (because that's how long it typically does take in the real world), I am going to ask them to send me the offer with 21 days on the contract and an extension for 9 days and another for 15 days. We will execute all three things at the same time, but we will not show the extensions to either the title company or the lender.

They will only receive the contract that gives them 21 days to be ready to close. This will force the lender to prioritize my deal. That means the lender will put in to get my lien search done more quickly by the title company, which will give me more time to get any issues resolved. It will also put the pressure on the lender to get this deal into and through underwriting as quickly as possible. With that I mix in a hefty dose of desperate follow-up to remind the lender, "You don't have a lot of time. We have to close this one fast" and "You told me you close these in 21 days." Will this behavior result in me burning in real estate hell? Depends on the person you ask, I guess. The title company and lender may say yes, but my customer loves it. To be clear, who is the person I was trying to close for life again?

The Lending Process

This is one where agents bleed potential credibility because they are too quick to outsource. Most agents have very little idea what lenders do to approve buyers for loans. Agents get the lead and send the buyers to the mortgage broker, the mortgage broker sends the buyers back with how much they can afford, and the agents get them a house and get paid. The thing is, as agents, we should thoroughly understand the lending process and tell our customers what to expect before they speak to the lender. When the lender tells the buyers pretty much everything we told them, how does that make us look? Do you think they feel like their agent understands the lending process?

If we could not speak authoritatively about the lending process, then all that credibility would go to the mortgage broker. Do you have the surplus "cred" to be giving it away like that? You want your customers to know that there isn't any part of this transaction that you don't understand and can't handle. Remember, the customers are scared. You knowing what the mortgage broker is doing gives them greater comfort that there are more eyes looking out for them. If you don't know the lender stuff, this is pretty easy to discover. Instead of giving the customers or the mortgage broker each other's contact info, arrange the call yourself, be on the call, listen, and learn.

Lack of Communication from the Other Side

Agents that don't or won't communicate is another black eye for our industry that every agent and customer complains about. If you are this agent, cut it out or leave the industry, please. You make life worse for everyone. No, it is not OK to say, "I only text." The code of ethics requires you to use your best efforts to help your customer. Not being able to push the little green button and talk to someone that may want to do a deal that benefits your customer does not qualify as your best effort even with the most generous of interpretations.

Letting our customers know that these kinds of agents exist is part of what we need to do. We also need to have a plan for how to deal with these agents, because sometimes when they don't respond, our customers think we are not reaching out to the agents enough. The way to handle these types of agents is the embarrassment method. It goes like this: You call and email them, and they don't respond. You wait a day or two and email them again; if they still don't respond, you send them another email copying their broker and blind-copying your customer. If there is still no response, you copy everyone else in the transaction (title company, mortgage broker, home inspector, the local dog catcher), and you start the email with, "This is my fifth attempt to reach you. You have not responded, and this behavior is not only unprofessional but also unethical." If that doesn't work, copy the attorney for your office as well. Sometimes seeing the @lawgroup lights a fire under people. If you are copying your customers on these emails, they know you are doing the work and fighting on their behalf.

OTHER WAYS TO BUILD CREDIBILITY

Out of respect for my customers' fear motivators, I need to do my pre-work. If I eat, live, sleep, and breathe real estate, it shouldn't be hard for me to demonstrate that I'm someone whose expertise is legitimate, and that I can handle whatever worries them. This is where the product knowledge we discussed in Part II gets implemented.

In any customer interaction, it is safe to assume the customer is interested in the real estate market. If that is the case, then I want to explain median home price, inflation numbers, gross domestic product, wages, unemployment, and all the other economic factors that most agents don't have as part of their knowledge arsenal. This helps to separate me from the image my customer has of the average agent.

While most agents are very good at telling you what is going on in the market, they are terrible at telling you why it's happening. That is like going to the doctor and saying, "Hey, doc, I think I've got a fever." The doctor takes out the thermometer and checks and says, "By Jove, you're right; you do have a fever." The doctor then proceeds to put away his medical equipment and hands you a bill. You say, "But, doc, why do you think I have the fever," and the doctor looks you right in the eye and says, "I have no idea, but here is my bill." You have to be able to tell people why.

The way to do this is to keep on top of what drives the national market and then adjust that understanding to your individual market. I want to be able to discuss what happens nationally and why our area will or will not follow the national trend. This shows the customers that you are looking at the trends, which gives them a sense that you have a feel for not just what is happening, but what will happen. If you know what is happening and what should happen based on the data, your customers can feel much more confident in their decision. This addresses their fear motivation directly and actually gives them what they want—a sense of confidence in what they should do.

There is one major caveat that has to be addressed in the modern practice of real estate. With all the sources of information out there, it is always possible that your customer could know more about a micro market than you do. An example of where you could run into this issue is if a customer wants to buy a unit in a certain condo building. The customer then researches that building for a year prior to contacting you. This is where you could lose a buyer to an agent that works exclusively in a building because of the agent's specific micro market knowledge. Even if that building was in your farm area, it is very tough to compete on the basis of specific building knowledge with an agent that focuses on one small area of the market exclusively.

The way to remedy this is to know the macro market really well. I know condos well, but I don't know each individual condo building. I also need to know how condos should perform compared with the rest of the market. Understanding the strengths and weaknesses of the condo market in your area, knowing the outlook for internal and external migration to that type of property (how many domestic and out-of-area buyers are coming), and being aware of any things that are going on in the larger market will give you a leg up on the myopic agent that just focuses on that one building.

My ability to tell my customers not only what's going on, but why it's happening, is critical for putting their mind at ease. Most customers fear making a mistake. If I can tell them what is going on and why, it gives them better data to assess and provides peace of mind with the decision they're making. This means my customers can enjoy their purchase more and worry less. Agents tend to spend a ton of time designing their business cards, and they forget that the real calling card they leave with the customer is the feeling the customer has about the experience of working with them. If they enjoy their transaction more, they are more likely to repeat that process.

Another important credibility-building tool is to have a stable of good-quality people that your customers may need at some point in the real estate process. This list is not limited to the usual suspects:

- Mortgage broker
- Home inspector
- Title company

You should also be on the lookout for:

- Real estate attorneys
- Probate attorneys
- Property management companies

- Handypersons
- General contractors
- Plumbers
- Electricians
- Locksmiths
- Landscapers
- Estate planning attorneys
- 1031 intermediaries
- Moving companies
- Folks that will pick up and remove furniture
- Accountants
- Water restoration folks
- Folks that fix violations and open permits

Having these folks to call upon shows your customers you are serious about providing them all the resources they might need.

Still, you want to do more than just have the people in your stable. You want to learn what your people do and be able to tell your customers what these folks will do before they speak to them. That way when your customers do speak with these folks and they back up what you told your customers, it shows your customers that you understand all facets of the business. If the customers trust you, and you know a whole lot more than just the real estate deal, does that also ease their mind knowing that you know enough to look out for them on these things too?

An example would be if someone told me that his mom died and left him her house. I would ask if there was a will and if it has gone through probate yet. If it hasn't, I would let him know what he needs to do to start the process. This is where I ask him if he has all the paperwork and tell him that in most cases, if everything looks good, he should be able to get this done in four to six months in my state. I explain, "That is a rough estimate though. You really need to speak to a probate attorney. Do you have one?" If he doesn't, I say, "OK, I have someone I can recommend. He charges $xxx per hour. What he probably will do is . . ." Then I explain what the standard procedure is and how this will or won't be the same, depending on his situation.

We expect this kind of informed advice in the outside world when dealing with a professional. Imagine you go to the doctor, and you have a broken arm. It is really bad, and the bone is sticking through the skin. You say, "Doc, this really hurts. Can you fix it?" The doctor says, "I'm sorry. I don't work on broken bones. You will need a specialist, and also, we aren't allowed to fix broken arms here at my office." You say, "OK, doc. Do you have someone you could recommend?" The doctor says, "I can do a Google search for someone, if you'd like." How would you feel about that doctor?

What about if we had the exact same scenario except after you say, "Doc, this really hurts. Can you fix it?," the doctor says, "I'm sorry. I am not allowed to work on broken bones for insurance reasons. You will need a specialist to look at that fracture. I happen to know one of the preeminent people in that field. I will call him and also the hospital down the street to get them to take you immediately. When you get there, they will probably do an x-ray or MRI to determine if there is anything floating in there that shouldn't be. They should then work on setting the bone if the imaging is clear. Barring some unforeseen issues, you should be in a lot less pain in about an hour to an hour and a half." Do you feel better or worse about this doctor?

Knowing not just what you do but also what the people you work with do gives the customers a sense of peace that you can watch out for them. My father always told me, "You should know what comes before and after what you do. It makes you better at what you do." Following this advice has served me very well (as has so much of my father's advice) in the real estate industry. This works well to establish your role for the customers as a market expert and an indispensable member of the team.

My broker once brought me in to work with a new customer. During our initial meeting, we had a great conversation about what makes a real estate market and the important factors to watch out for. That was the credibility negotiation. I showed him that I knew my stuff. Then I backed it up with facts, numbers, and action. I found a property that matched his interest and analyzed it for him. I gave him the differential cash flow, projected growth, etc., and explained the whole thing. He was blown away. When he needed vendors to get things done, I had the people, and they were good at what they did. Now, whenever he gets a piece of real estate anywhere in the country, he asks his team, "Has Josh Cadillac looked at it yet?" and "What does he think?" He's a customer for life, because he knows that he can trust me to keep up on the knowledge that sets me apart from other agents. That kind of customer isn't found. That's the kind of customer we are in this business to make.

EMPATHY = TRUST

When I was a little kid, one of my favorite things to do with my dad was to go to the movies. He was older and had worked hard most of his life, so his body was too banged up to play sports with me or anything, so the movies became our big thing to do together. There were three major life lessons my father taught at the movies: one when we were going into the theater, another when we were on the inside of the theater, and the third lesson when we were on the way out. These lessons come together to make up the core of the third of our big three things. No one in real estate told me these things, and I only learned them because a father wanted to pass on the lessons learned over a long hard lifetime.

TRUST

The first lesson was when we walked into the movie house from the parking lot. My father would tell me to hold his hand because I was small and cars couldn't see me, so that was how to stay safe. He would grab my hand, shake my arm, and say, "You see that? That's how fast an accident can happen."

The lesson wasn't about parking lot navigation. It was found in the experience I had when I gave my dad my hand, which was complete trust. I knew my dad would jump in front of a bus before he would let anything hurt me. My dad had shown me that he could be trusted, and because of that I would follow him anywhere. I didn't look at the traffic or the cars because I knew my dad would navigate me through and was always looking out for me. This showed me how important trust is in a relationship, and the freedom you feel when you are in the hands of someone you completely trust.

"Trust" is a word that is thrown around in real estate all the time, and so we need to make sure we are clear on the trust we mean. Customers "trusting" you to have the key to their house and believing you won't steal something is not what we are talking about. We are also not discussing the customers listening to your advice either. The trust we need here is like the trust I had with my dad. Do your customers know that you will do what's best for them even if it is not best for you? Will you give them the advice that reflects what you would do? Or will you give them the advice that earns you a commission? Most customers think the answer is the latter. They treat agents like mercenaries. They do this because most agents behave like mercenaries.

EMPATHY

The second lesson was given when we got inside at the best time of the moviegoing experience—candy time! I would see all the kids put their face and hands against the glass of the candy display. They would try to get as close to the candy as possible, smooshing themselves against the glass like one of those suction-cup Garfield dolls people used to have in their cars. To my four-year-old mind, it almost seemed like the closer they got to the candy, the sooner it would be in their mouth or something. When I got to the counter to test this candy-proximity-to-consumption hypothesis, my father grabbed my hand and said, "Son, don't touch the glass. If you touch the glass, it will make handprints, and someone will have to clean it." What I learned from this was the importance of empathy. There are other people in the world, and they matter. I need to consider them when doing things.

This is a lesson I forgot when I was a young guy first entering the dating pool. I remember being discouraged when I'd try to talk to a girl and she would respond in a rude way. "Why was she so rude to me? Is it something about me?" I lamented to my friends. To which my friends of course responded, "Yes, you suck." (But discussing how the males of the species take pride in their ability to "rip" on each other is a topic for another book.) Then someone said something I had never considered before, and it changed things for me forever. A friend of mine said, "Did you ever consider what it is like to be her"? He reminded me that women get approached all the time. Without anything to make me stand out, the perception was that I was just another dude with a cheesy line. This was very generous of my friend, as I had forgotten my father's advice to think of the other person and had just thought about things from my perspective. The girl I was trying to talk to simply didn't want to be bothered with the same old crap. When I thought about it, I couldn't blame her.

The American consumer is like the young woman at the bar. We are being sold to all the time. Think about pharmaceutical marketing, overly zealous salespeople at the mall, and even those targeted advertisements on social media. We can spot salespeople a mile away, and we're not usually happy with their presence. And I get it. Most people in sales don't spend much time thinking about anyone other than themselves; they just want that commission. Empathy makes us consider what the experience of others would be like by putting ourselves in their shoes and asking, "What would I want if I was where they are?" This is a question agents do not ask nearly enough. Their presentations are designed around what they want to say, rather than what the customer needs to hear. They give customers answers that they think answer the question, but their answers do not connect the dots for a non–real estate professional, like a customer.

Here are a few examples of this:

Bad presentation. A self-aggrandizing presentation based on displaying the agent's accomplishments, awards, time on market, etc.
Good presentation. A market-based presentation based on the customers' fears that shows them that their needs were considered and addressed.

Bad answer. Customer: "Why do you want to put a lockbox on our property?"
Agent: "To make it easier to show."
Good answer. Customer: "Why do you want to put a lockbox on our property"?
Agent: "Because, Mr. and Mrs. Seller, the people showing this property are real estate agents, and as it turns out, I am one too. I know that when it is time to schedule to show properties, it always provides a sense of relief when we see a property on lockbox because it means we have access to the property without someone having to be in the house to let us in. This makes it easy for us to show the house, and it also allows for flexibility in the showing schedule. Sometimes customers take longer in properties than we thought or vice versa. This makes agents either late or early for appointments, and it can be a mess. For this reason, having a couple of properties on lockbox that can be accessed earlier or later allows the schedule to flex. What this means is that the lockbox properties always get shown more frequently. If this property is shown more frequently, we should receive more offers on it. If we receive more offers, we will have more negotiating power. If we have more negotiating power, we can get to

a higher final sale price. So, the reason I want a lockbox on this home is to make you more money, Mr. and Mrs. Seller."

Yes, the good answer is longer. You took the time to explain it fully to your customers so you could show them how you are truly looking out for their best interests. As it turns out, the customers thinking you are looking out for them is really helpful in making them want to continue being your customer.

UNDERSTAND THE IMPACT
OF YOUR ACTIONS

The third lesson my dad taught me at the movie theater was when we would walk out the door. As a little kid, I would walk out the door and just let it go without looking behind me. One day I did that, and my dad banged the door with his fist, and when I turned around, he acted like the door had hit him in the head. I felt really bad. I thought I had hurt my dad. He then told me that it hadn't hit him, but it easily could have. He said that my actions had the ability to help or genuinely hurt people if I wasn't paying attention. I have a responsibility to humanity to be responsible and considerate of others and to make sure my actions do not hurt them. We are in this thing together.

There is an empathy component here, but it also ties into responsibility and the sense that the actions I take to get what I want (leave the theater) may have bad consequences for other people. One of the places this lesson manifests in real estate is when agents ask investor customers how much they have to spend and then try to find them a property at that price. The agents see the dollar signs and do not check to make sure they aren't "slamming the door" on their customers. One of the biggest drawbacks of investing in real estate is the lack of liquidity. In other words, if you need cash today and are holding nothing but real estate, you are screwed.

A question you should always ask an investor is, how is your access to cash? Do you have liquid cash available besides this money you are planning to invest in real estate? I always tell the customers that I want to make sure that if they find themselves short on money, there is capital available to them. If they are using all their money to buy, I encourage them to reduce what they plan to invest in real estate and instead invest some of the money into something with greater liquidity. Yes, it reduces my commission. It also makes sure that my customers don't get overextended, and that makes them more likely to be happy with their real estate investment.

ALWAYS LOOK OUT FOR THE CUSTOMERS

So, how do you show your customers that you're different from their preconceived notion of a salesperson? You need to make the case that you are looking out for them. One of the things I do is say, "Look, folks. Luckily, I don't need to do this deal to eat today. What I want to do is give you as much information as I can about this process. That way, you're prepared to be the best customer you can be, because you're informed. Whether you choose to work with me or someone else, no one is going to pull the wool over your eyes." That last line is important; giving people permission to walk away is powerful. For me, these words are genuine. A lot of salespeople actually are smart. A lot of them trip all over themselves to be likable. Nothing special there. But what locks in customers for life is believing that you're looking out for them. And the reason they should believe it is because you *are*.

Here's an example. Rude people suck, right? In real estate there is often this "us versus them" mindset that develops because of how agents perceive being slighted by the customers. I was talking to an agent one day after a class I taught, and she asked me for advice. She told me about this tough customer—a former attorney who had given her a house to sell that belonged to his son. It turns out the son went to jail, and so the parents who bought him this house decided to sell it. The parents had the proper paperwork to do the deal, but despite the agent bringing several good offers to them, the attorney father was being very unreasonable with his demands. This caused several of the offers to fall through, and the agent to get very frustrated. She then told me that the son was getting out of prison sooner than expected and that she thought the sellers were just waiting for the listing agreement to expire in order to take it off the market. She was hurt, angry, and fed up with the sellers and told me she was ready to fire the couple before they got a chance to fire her.

I told her this is an example of what happens when you forget the big picture. Do you want this deal, or all the other deals they will ever do? She said she wasn't sure she wanted these customers anymore. I asked her what the best thing would be that she could do to show them that she was looking out for them. She said she didn't know and asked me what I would do. I said I would call them immediately and tell them I heard their son was getting out of jail and offer my congratulations. I would then offer to immediately remove the listing from the MLS if that's what they wanted me to do, as I'm here to do whatever is best for them. I don't want to sell this house if they still may need it.

I told her if they were going to fire you anyway, then this costs you nothing. You will, however, gain trust for showing them that your commission is a secondary thought, and you are considering them first. I told her to stop looking at the customers as if they were adversaries, but instead like the people who trusted her with their business. Try not to view this from her side, but to get on the same side of the table as her customers and view the situation like a trusted advisor would. She needed to answer the question, "If I were in their shoes, what would be the best advice I could give them to help them reach their goals?"

I had the opportunity to go back to teach in the same location about two months later, and the same agent was in attendance. She excitedly told me what happened. The relationship with the customer dramatically improved. The son got out of jail, but when she offered to remove the listing, the parents reassured her that they still wanted to sell. The father became a bit more reasonable and trusting to work with, and the property is under contract. The parents even discussed giving her their multimillion-dollar home to list in the future. She got on their side and showed them that she works to get *them* their best outcome, not hers. It resulted in a better outcome than she had hoped for. This doesn't always happen that way, but you know what? She can sure as hell look herself in the mirror at night. She knows the type of business she runs. She does the right thing and looks out for her customers. There is a value in deciding on and adhering to the terms by which you conduct your life and run your business.

TRUST BUILDING

Trust building is the hardest of our big three things to earn. I'm going to give you a couple of examples of how to use some common scenarios to try to score points in the trust column. These will tend to come through when you know what your business is about and you have prepared responses that reflect your best efforts at providing your customers with service they can't find elsewhere.

Getting Preapproved

Here is one for the buyer's side that can be done a lot better than the way I currently hear agents do this. When customers ask agents why they should get preapproved, agents say things that sound good to them, but their customers hear differently. Let me do some interpreting of some common answers I hear agents give to this question:

Customer asks: "Why should I get preapproved?"

Agent says: "So we don't waste your time showing you houses you can't afford."
Customer thinks: "'Cause you're lazy and don't want to waste your time."

Agent says: "So you don't miss out on your dream home if you find it."
Customer thinks: "You don't think I can afford it and don't want to waste your time."

Agent says: "So you know what you can afford."
Customer thinks: "So you can get me to spend more than I want to."

There are more than just these, but I think you get the general drift. The agents' statements make sense and are not wrong on the face of things, but why are we saying things like this? Is it to say what needs saying? Or is it to make sure what needs to be heard and understood is heard and understood? If we want to get our customers motivated to do what's in their best interest, we need to align our answers clearly with something they care about.

I tell customers the reason they want to get preapproved is because it makes their offer less risky to the seller. I start by saying, "Assume you are the seller and two offers come in. One offer is cash for $400,000, and one is with a financing contingency and is also for $400,000. If all other terms are the same, which offer would you select"? They will always say, "The cash offer." I then ask, "What if the finance offer was $401,000 and the cash one stayed the same; you would probably stick with the cash offer still?" When they answer yes, I respond, "What if the finance offer went to $405,000 or $410,000 at some point. You would consider the finance offer better than the cash offer, correct"? They say "Correct." I then ask, "What did the finance offer have to do to be better than the cash one?" They say, "It had to pay."

So here's how I wrap my response: "That's the problem, Mr. and Mrs. Buyer. If we put in this riskier offer, it is going to make our offer weaker. If our offer is weaker, it means we will have to pay more than an identical offer that simply has reduced that risk for the seller. If there is one thing that will eat my soul, it is that any customer of mine ever has to pay one nickel more to buy a piece of property because of something we could have fixed in advance. Mr. and Mrs. Buyer, I want you to get preapproved because I don't want to see you spend any more for your house than you absolutely need to."

This has a credibility component to it that I think is pretty clear. In addition, it has the benefit of allowing me to tell the customer things like "Your paying more would make me lose sleep." This shows them what my business is about and that I am fighting to save them money. I want this because I know how this works and this is how to get you what you really want at the best possible price.

Keeping Good Tenants Is Good for Business

One of my businesses is a property management company. Often the landlords call me near renewal time to ask how much the market rent is. If there is a big jump in the rent, they will ask what I think they should take the rent to. There is a bit of a potential conflict of interest for me here, because if the existing tenant leaves, the customer will give me the rental listing. The natural incentive is to get the existing tenant to leave so that I can rerent the place and get paid a commission. For this reason, I always try to do just the opposite and recommend a conservative price increase. I always ask if the tenant is a good tenant. If the tenant is, I tell the landlord it is worth it to keep a good tenant to avoid the vacancy, the rental commission, and the risk that the next tenant might be a problem.

Does this reduce my bottom line? In the short run, definitely. In the long run though, these customers have stayed with my management company for years. They always call me first if they want to buy more property, and they have sent numerous other customers to me. This has eliminated my need to spend money and time to advertise. In the long run, hands down this is the right play.

Refinance and Don't Sell

I had a customer call to tell me that his mom was sick and he might need to sell the investment property I helped him buy seven years earlier. The first thing I said to him was, "Jeez, I'd hate to see you sell that place. It has been such a great producer. Have you thought about refinancing it?" To be clear, if he refinances, I make zero.

The call went on for a while, and for about 20 minutes I argued for the benefits of doing the refinance. It wasn't that I didn't want the listing. This property would have sold in a nanosecond. But that didn't even cross my mind. I was just trying to figure out the best way to get him the money he needed and leave him in the best possible position. At some point, I said to him, "You do realize that for the last 20 minutes I have been trying to talk you out of giving me a commission, right?" He said, "I know that, Josh, and that's why I love you and why you are the only guy I call."

There are plenty more stories I could share of how developing trust with a customer pays off, but I think the important thing to realize here is this: If the customers had a lamp they rubbed and a genie popped out and said, "What would you like in a real estate agent?," what would they say? Answering that question is something every agent should do before ever showing a property.

Or to ask in a different way: "Who are the customers, and what do they want from me?" The simple answer is they want someone they like, who knows what the hell he or she is doing and is looking out for them. If you give your customers that, they will have no reason to ever look for another agent, and plenty of reasons to refer you to everyone they meet that needs real estate help.

PART IV

BUILD A BUSINESS YOU'RE PROUD OF

CHAPTER 15

COMPLETING THE CLOSE FOR LIFE

The deal is finalized. You have your commission, and your customers are happily lounging by the pool in their new home. Is your relationship with them over? For most agents, the answer is, "Yes, baby! I got paid. I am out of here!" If you want to Close for Life (and probably get a lot more fulfillment out of your work), the answer is no. Those customers should continue to matter to you. After all, of all the salespeople out there, they made a choice to work with *you*. That's a privilege that shouldn't be taken for granted.

There are many ways to show customers that they still matter. Staying in contact, for one. More than 80 percent of customers can't remember the agent's name after two years. People have a lot on their mind and are busy, and if you don't stay in contact, you can easily be forgotten. Don't think that just automating and reaching out to them in constant contact or using Mailchimp is enough.

The industry is fascinated by the number of times you need to "touch" people to get their business. I don't know that there's a right answer to that, but I do know that ending up in the customer's email trash file doesn't help.

Instead of sending customers an email that most of us would delete so quickly it might cause a sonic boom on our phone, how about we try communicating in a way customers find more meaningful?

In my business, that method is picking up the phone and calling customers to check in. I don't call to sell them real estate. I call to let them know they matter to me and the deal(s) they entrusted me with is a part of the reason I have built the business that I have today. These folks are what got me here. Yes, I worked hard and did all I could to give them superior service, but nothing happens without the customers. So, I call them and tell them I was thinking of them and wanted to see how they were doing. I do this four times a year for each customer. Why? Two reasons: one, because they deserve it, and two, because your competitors are too lazy or self-absorbed to commit to doing it.

There are lots of ways to show the public you run a different kind of business. You can throw annual parties for past customers, like a barbeque at a park. This can help foster a tribe mentality and help keep you in the front of their mind. You can do handwritten notes, remember birthdays and anniversaries, and reach out. Notice these are things that go far beyond a closing gift. That tends to be the kiss-off from the agent that says, "We got you across the finish line; now you are on your own." The closing is just the end of the beginning. You need to consistently remind your customers that you do what you do differently and better than what they are used to. Don't give them a chance to forget that.

My chiropractor is a great example of this. I began to see him years ago at the recommendation of a friend who had been in a bad car wreck. "This guy completely fixed me. He's who you need to see," he told me. I was ready to try anything. I had been suffering from such severe neck pain that I actually went to see the Miami Dolphins' surgeon. He told me that my days of doing shoulder presses at the gym were over and to contact him when the pain reached a certain threshold, at which point he would do surgery.

After my first visit with the chiropractor, he asked me what I wanted to be able to do. Thinking I was asking for the world, I told him that I'd love to be able to do shoulder presses again at some point. He considered my x-rays and said, "Three months." I told him, "Now, my workouts aren't the Jane Fonda five-pound weight type. I'm used to lifting big dumbbells." He said something to the effect of, "You'll be able to put a house over your head when I'm done with you." Three months later he proved true to his word; I was doing shoulder presses again and was pain-free.

This chiropractor had already shown me that he knew his stuff, but he really completed the Close for Life when my brother came to visit and told me he was in tremendous pain. I immediately called my chiropractor and asked if my brother could see him. He said that he likely wouldn't be able to take my brother's insurance but that he should show up twice a day for the week while he was in town. If the insurance pays, great. If not, fine too. He just genuinely wanted to help this guy who was suffering. My brother went, and the chiropractor adjusted him twice a day for a week with no guarantee of payment. That was something very different from what I expected.

In our ever-changing world of machines and artificial intelligence, the business owners who hold tight to the idea that human interaction is essential are the ones that will differentiate themselves within the market. Even long after my own pain is gone, and my chiropractor has moved farther away, I drive past dozens of other chiropractors to get to this guy. I have referred dozens of people to him and would never even think of referring a friend to anyone but him. He has earned all my business and completed the Close for Life.

That's it, folks. It's pretty simple. The customers matter, and they want someone who treats them like they do. Agents say they do that all the time, but their actions don't bear that out. The reason for this is maintaining standards is hard. It requires taking the road less traveled, and that scares people away. The thing is, that less traveled road forces you to build and run a business in a way that you can be proud of; that upholds your commitment to yourself and your customer; and that makes your work feel more important to you. In this life where so many struggle to find purpose, this way of doing business does far more than just help you build a business. By closing your customers for life, you are pursuing the happiness the founders of were talking about and doing business in a way that makes your life and work as meaningful as possible.

ACKNOWLEDGMENTS

So many folks have contributed in so many ways and helped more than they know (including putting up with me). I hope I'm not forgetting anyone, but am sure I am. Thank you to my mom, Joie, my dad, Bob, Tim, Dominique, Lili Padilla, Valeria Cornejo, Cody Lampariello, K.B., Jesus Castanon, Drew Epstein, Eddie Petasne, Galen H., Alex B., Cherolyne, Lisa Betts, Steve Carlis, Carly Evans and the 2MM team, Cheryl Segura, Kevin Commins, and all the good folks at McGraw Hill and Betts Works Inc., Chubasaur, and for God's amazing grace that has always seen me through.

INDEX

ABOUT
THE AUTHOR

Josh Cadillac is a top-producing real estate agent, coach, national keynote speaker, and author who trains professionals how to close for life by building lasting success through extensive knowledge. His unique method combines the education that salespeople need to survive in their industry with the tools to convert that knowledge into rapport, credibility, and trust. Josh has earned many of the most prestigious certifications and designations in the industry and was recently recognized as Speaker of the Year by Miami Realtors.

Josh has written numerous courses on various facets of real estate in his A.C.E. family of classes, including the first crypto and real estate course approved for continuing education in Florida—and only the third one approved anywhere in the United States. Josh's teaching focuses on the real-world skills that agents need to be true advocates and trusted resources for their customers. His goal is to make the most of agents' time while teaching them to take their business personally and grow it to the next level. He believes in counting success not in paychecks received but in satisfied customers that won't ever do business with anyone else.

Josh runs his business with his family under the watchful eye of their English bulldog, Chubasaur, who is responsible for all quality control issues.